PRAISE FOR *EVERYTHING YO* *ABOUT RENTING BUT DIDN'T KNOW TO ASK*

"Sadly, most renters still struggle to find a rental that will welcome their pets today. In this book, Bordo and Hildebolt help pet owners understand why it is often difficult to find a rental that includes pets, and they explain what you can do to be more successful in the search for a home. It's essential reading for any renter who has or wants a pet."

–Judy Bellack, Michelson Found Animals and the Pet-Inclusive Housing Initiative

"Most young people rent their first apartment and sign a lease with no guidance whatsoever on how to be a renter. This book should be required reading for every first-time renter (or even those who have rented before) to understand their rights, avoid scams, and get the most value out of their rental experience. It walks the aspiring renter through applications, leases, tenant rights, budgeting, and much more."

–Deidre Woollard, Editor/Producer, The Motley Fool

"I've helped more than a thousand renters find new homes and apartments, and I wish I'd been able to give them all this book. It's filled with practical information and acts as a map to the world of rentals. It's a wealth of knowledge and the transparency it provides makes the renting experience more secure, enjoyable, and successful for renters."

–Jasmine Ward, Realtor/Owner, Honey Home Ltd

"Finally there's a book to help all of us who struggle with the rental search. It's never been easy to find a great rental. Dwellsy's book *Everything You Need to Know About Renting* is an absolute must-read for anyone looking to navigate the complex and often overwhelming world of rental searching. With clear, concise advice and insider tips, this book is a valuable resource for anyone looking to find their perfect rental home. I really think that the authors' wealth of knowledge and experience in the rental industry shines through on every page, making it easy for readers to understand and apply the strategies outlined in the book. Whether you're a first-time renter or a seasoned pro, this book is sure to help you be successful in your rental search. I'm excited to give the book to my son to help him when he needs to find a place too! I highly recommend it!"

–Nancy Pacheco, Renter and Dwellsy user

"I think what has impressed me the most about Jonas is his intentional prioritization of the renting experience from the perspective of the tenant and this book is that next resource. It's a guide, a reference, and a narrative, all focused on providing renters with the best tools to craft their rental experiences. Phenomenal!"

–Deandra McDonald, Real Estate Investor

"Finding a rental is the biggest financial decision that a renter makes each year, and sadly, it's a challenging process full of pitfalls and risks. *Everything You Need to Know About Renting* is exactly what's been needed to help renters: an insider's guide to the rental process that arms the reader with the information they need to both land a great place and make the most of their home."

–Tom Loverro, Board Director, NerdWallet

"Renting a home can mean so many different things, from a resort-like experience to suffering through a slumlord, and Jonas Bordo and Hannah Hildebolt do a phenomenal job of explaining how to find a perfect scenario. By understanding how people can become 'accidental landlords' to seeing the pros and cons to giant, national property managers, this book provides readers with a quick way to better understand what type of home is best for them."

–Brent Williams, Chief Insider, Multifamily Insiders

"As a first-time renter, I'm so glad that I now have the information from this guide to take with me for the future. Bordo and Hildebolt provide both practical tips for finding and maintaining a rental and an overall context to the rental structure, like how renting from an individual landlord versus a management company might result in a different experience. This book would make a great gift for the new renters in your life."

–Johanna Zenn, Renter and Dwellsy User

"Bordo and Hildebolt craft an accessible and engaging guide for those stepping into the rental market for the first time. This book would have made my first apartment search so much less daunting. It's loaded with helpful advice, from its insight into the market as a whole to its many practical tools. The decision matrix in particular would have helped my roommates and I discuss our priorities. This book armed me with knowledge I wouldn't have even known to seek out."

–Victoria Bonacasa, Renter and Dwellsy User

EVERYTHING YOU NEED TO KNOW ABOUT RENTING BUT DIDN'T KNOW TO ASK

EVERYTHING YOU NEED TO KNOW ABOUT RENTING BUT DIDN'T KNOW TO ASK

All the Insider Dirt to Help You Get the Best Deal and Avoid Disaster

From the Renting Experts at Dwellsy

Jonas Bordo

with Hannah Hildebolt

Matt Holt Books
An Imprint of BenBella Books, Inc.
Dallas, TX

This book is designed to provide accurate and authoritative information about the residential rental process. Neither the author nor the publisher is engaged in rendering legal, accounting, or other professional services by publishing this book. If any such assistance is required, the services of a qualified professional should be sought. The author and publisher will not be responsible for any liability, loss, or risk incurred as a result of the use and application of any information contained in this book.

Matt Holt is an imprint of BenBella Books, Inc.
10440 N. Central Expressway
Suite 800
Dallas, TX 75231
benbellabooks.com
Send feedback to feedback@benbellabooks.com

BenBella and *Matt Holt* are federally registered trademarks.

Printed in the United States of America
10 9 8 7 6 5 4 3 2 1

Library of Congress Control Number: 2022060012
ISBN 9781637743928 (trade paperback)
ISBN 9781637743935 (electronic)

Editing by Katie Dickman
Copyediting by Lydia Choi
Proofreading by Jenny Bridges and Ashley Casteel
Indexing by WordCo.
Text design and composition by Aaron Edmiston
Cover design and illustration by Garrett Zuiderweg
Printed by Lake Book Manufacturing

FOR RENTERS EVERYWHERE AND THE AMAZING DWELLSY TEAM THAT MOVES HEAVEN AND EARTH EACH DAY TO SERVE THEM.

Contents

SECTION 3: YOUR UNIQUE RENTAL SITUATION

SECTION 4: MOVING IN AND MAKING THE MOST OF YOUR PLACE

SECTION 5: RENEWING AND MOVING ON

Let's Get Started

You're alone in your new place. Truly alone.

And there's just no other way to put this: it's a mess.

In the bedroom, your bed is assembled, and the desk and bookshelf, too. The dresser is still in its IKEA box in a corner. The rug on the ground is an old one, but it's much loved and passed to you from your grandmother.

There's a partially assembled bookshelf in the living room, next to a TV on its stand and a dining-room table missing its chairs but topped with a lone piece of garlic and pepperoni pizza in a nearly empty box, left by your friends before departing. There's nowhere to sit.

In the open kitchen, there are stacked dishes, pots and pans, and glasses waiting to be assigned to a cupboard.

Moving boxes are *everywhere*—the hallway, the living room, the kitchen, the bedroom, the bathroom. There are two garbage bags on the floor of the closet filled with clothes you didn't take time to box up.

The light is fading, and from your bedroom window, you have a view of the city. With a beer in your hand, sitting in the desk chair from your childhood bedroom, you watch the sun go down, and it's stunning. Maybe the most beautiful view you've ever seen. And not because it's the most amazing scenery in the world or the best view in history, but because it's yours. All yours. For the first time in your life, you have your very own place. Maybe the road's been bumpy, or maybe things went more smoothly than you'd ever hoped. However it went, it's over now. You've found your first rental.

Or maybe it's not your first time—maybe it's your second, or your third, or your tenth move. Maybe you're looking for ways to make the rental process smoother because you're sick of stressing out about it. We're here to help you, too.

Either way, you can do this. Together, we can get you there. Let's get started.

WHO ARE WE?

Before we get started, we imagine you'll want to know a little more about your guides. We are Jonas and Hannah from Dwellsy, the nation's preeminent marketplace for rental housing. Collectively, we have more than thirty years of experience in renting and rentals, but if we're being completely straight with you, Jonas has most of those years—he's the old guy in this outfit.

Jonas is the CEO and cofounder of Dwellsy and has been around the rental business for many years. He's been a renter many, many times, and he's been a landlord, too, both on a small scale and a huge scale—he was once responsible for sixty thousand apartments.

He's taken that insider knowledge and put it to use to build Dwellsy and to help renters get an edge in finding a great place to live more quickly, more easily, and more safely.

Hannah—the younger one in this outfit—has been with Dwellsy since nearly the beginning. Currently, she's housed in New York City's massive and endlessly complicated rental market. Mostly, she writes and edits content for Dwellsy's blog, although her work can also be found across Dwellsy's website and social accounts. In other words, Hannah is a big part of Dwellsy's voice, particularly when it comes to the company's long-form content. Thanks to all of the time she's spent writing for renters, Hannah has developed a robust knowledge of the rental industry. She knows how to break the rental world down into clear, accessible language, and that's her goal throughout this book. When Hannah combines her talents with Jonas's deep experience, real magic happens. That's how this book came about. Together, we've teamed up to guide you through all things rental.

HOW TO USE THIS BOOK

If you're new to renting and looking for (or dreaming of) your very first place, then we recommend starting at the beginning and reading through the book from front to back. Here's how the book is organized:

- Section 1 gives you everything you need to know about the rental world, including why your landlord thinks the way they do, why there are so many scammers targeting you when you go out to look for a rental, and more.
- Section 2 walks you through the full process for the rental search. It shows you how to navigate the search from the very first steps all the way to that successful goal—you, happy in your own place!
- Section 3 is all about how to handle unique situations. Say you need a pet, or maybe a roommate. Maybe you need a place within an incredibly short span of time. Or maybe you're a college student looking for off-campus housing, and you're not sure how to find it. We all have a specific set of circumstances, and they all require that you bring something special to the rental search.
- Section 4 is about how to make the most of your current place. Once you've found it, how do you make your place great? How do you keep the peace with your landlord and your neighbors? How do you make your rental reflect your personality?
- Section 5 is about ending the lease and moving on. Even ending a lease and moving out can be done to your advantage. Among other things, let's help you get your security deposit back.

If you're an experienced renter and you're looking for insider secrets, feel free to hop around and cherry-pick the topics that look most interesting or most relevant to you. To a significant degree, this book is intended to be a reference guide that you can turn to for guidance over the course of your renting life.

Section 1

MASTERING THE WEIRD WORLD OF RENTALS

We want you to win at your apartment search. That means getting a place that's great for you—one that fits within your budget and suits your needs and those of your loved ones.

A big part of winning at renting is understanding the world of rentals and why folks do the things they do. That means understanding landlords, supers, scammers, and all the other personalities that inhabit this world.

Spoiler alert: it's a bit of a weird world with its own idiosyncrasies. But, after all, that's why we wrote this book—to help you find the best next place for you.

This section will help you understand:

- Landlords and what drives them
- How to avoid getting scammed (22 percent of renters get scammed. Don't be one of them!)
- The types of places available to rent

Why start here and not just by looking at places? Because we want you to be successful in the search, and a little knowledge will go a long way in helping arm you for success in the search to come.

Plus—and this is really important—the inventory of rental homes and apartments changes constantly, and what's available today *will* be gone tomorrow. If you're not completely prepared when you encounter your dream place, you'll not only lose it, but you'll also waste time and money chasing it.

It's better to do a little work beforehand and put yourself in a position to win.

1.1

RENTING VS. BUYING

RENTING IS A GREAT CHOICE FOR MOST OF US

Here in the United States, our culture is incredibly focused on owning your own home, and you may have that as a goal, too. It's a goal for millions of people across the country, and it's been ingrained in many of us as a measure of success.

Hear us out, though: home ownership doesn't have to be the default.

"What's wrong with owning a home?" you're wondering. "I want my own place!" We know, we know. We're not knocking it. Home ownership is right for some people. It might be the perfect solution for you. It's just not the right fit for everyone all the time.

It takes a lot of money to buy a home. It also takes a lot of time and energy to maintain a home—more than you might think. If it sounds like these things won't be problems for you, then maybe you're cut out to be a homeowner.

But lots of us don't have extra time, money, and energy. We just want a nice, affordable place to live in a location we love, a place where things run smoothly. If that sounds good to you, we're here to present you with an alternative option: renting. Renting can be even better than owning a home. It's sustainable, flexible, and it can even be downright exciting.

Willing to let us make our case? Let's jump in.

1. **Renting Is Good for Your Wallet**

We know that renting can feel like just throwing money away, but home ownership actually fits that description a lot better. NerdWallet did a study demonstrating how expensive owning a home can be compared to renting.[1] Turns out owning a home costs more than renting in every single state in America. In the pricier markets, it's as much as 90 percent more expensive. Yikes.

You've probably heard that owning a home is a way to build wealth. Some people do sell their homes for more money than they originally paid for them. However, that doesn't include all of the maintenance, property taxes, and home insurance they paid over the years to own the home in question. When you add up all of those things, home ownership is often definitely not a sound financial decision.

2. **Renting Saves Time**

Money isn't the only thing you'll save by renting. Renting also saves a ton of time when compared to home ownership. Think about the maintenance it takes to keep up an entire home. The drains, the gutters, the pipes, the roofing, even just the lawn—all of these are your responsibility to take care of as a homeowner. (Cleaning gutters! Fun!) While you may save time if you hire someone else to do the work for you, you'll end up spending a lot of money.

If you rent, you won't have to worry about this kind of routine maintenance. These things, and many more, are a landlord's responsibility. You can just sit back and enjoy your rental and spend your time on the things you're passionate about, which we're guessing doesn't include cleaning the gutters!

3. **Renting Is Flexible**

Imagine that you get your dream job offer. There's only one teeny, tiny hitch: it's in another city or another state, even. If you want to take it, you'll have to move. It's not an unheard-of scenario in a world where half of all Americans who move do so for work.[2]

If you're ever in that situation, a house will tie you down to one place like nothing else. Selling can be a long, complicated process, and homeowners don't always come out on top. As recently as late 2022, enormous increases in interest rates have caused homeowners to lose their homes because of falling home prices combined with a doubling of interest rates, which almost doubles the cost of a mortgage and puts it out of reach for many, including those who've already bought their home and just need to refinance it. And this isn't the first time homeowners have seen this kind of brutal loss—something similar, but worse, happened in 2009 as a result of a house price bubble and easy access to bad mortgages.

In fact, it generally takes seven to ten years to get enough appreciation on a property to pay for the costs associated with selling a home, so lots of homeowners lose money on their place if they need to sell before that—and now, twice in two decades, market conditions have caused waves of homeowner losses and bankruptcies.

As a renter, you won't have to deal with any of that. You can usually tell your landlord you're leaving and work things out by paying some extra rent, even if your lease isn't ending soon. If it is, all the better: no extra rent necessary.

Renting sounds pretty good, right? It's not just a great choice for many people—it's also the smart choice for many of us.

Remember: Renting is a great—and smart—choice for most people at many points in their lives. Always make your housing choice work for you.

1.2

INSIDE THE MIND OF THE LANDLORD

A big part of being a renter and getting and keeping a great place is understanding the mystery that is your landlord.

For many of us, the landlord seems like an abstract authority figure, well removed from anything we know.

Getting to know who they are and where they're coming from can be a big help to you in this process, so it's well worth your time.

To begin, there are three types of landlords in the United States:

1. **Individual landlords.** These are individuals just like you, except they own a rental property. These folks own and operate about 50 percent of all rentals, and if you're looking at a single-family home or a condo, it's most likely to be owned and managed by someone like this.
2. **Corporate owner/operators.** These are companies that own and operate rental properties. They are both the owner and the operator of the rental properties. These companies own and operate about 15 percent of all rentals.

3. **Third-party property managers.** These are companies, large or small, who manage properties for others. They aren't the owner; they manage the property for the owner. These folks manage about 35 percent of all rentals.

Why does it matter which type of landlord you might have? Well, the type of landlord will make a big difference in how you interact with them, the timing and quality of the response you'll receive if there is a problem, and their approach to taking care of your home.

Let's dig into each type of landlord, understanding that we're going to make some generalizations based on what we've observed about their behaviors. There are more than ten million individual landlords and tens of thousands of property managers and owner/operators, and all are different.

LANDLORD TYPE #1: INDIVIDUAL LANDLORDS

One way to think about this group is that most of them are, believe it or not, "accidental" landlords.

How so? Well, often, they became a landlord when someone passed away and they inherited a property. Or, they moved to another location and didn't sell their old place, perhaps because they were not there long enough to break even and would lose money if they sold. Maybe they thought they were going to move back, or they just didn't feel the timing was right. In many—or even most—cases, they didn't set out to become landlords, and they're not property-management professionals. They're just doing the best they can.

There's a ton of variation in terms of how these landlords approach management of their rentals and how well (or poorly) positioned they are to be a great landlord for you.

They may live close to your place or far away. If they're close, that makes it easy for them to come over and check on the property to deal with things as they come up. If they're further away, they may need to rely on you more to let them know when something needs to be done.

They may have lots of money to take care of things, or they may not. This can be a thorny one. Of course, as the one living in the property, you would love the landlord to spend all the money in the world to make your home amazing. Unfortunately, just like you, your landlord has to live within their means, and that means they have to cover all of the costs of the property—mortgage, insurance, taxes, and maintenance—which, together, are often more than the rent that you're paying on the place.

They may know how to fix things themselves, or they may not. For a period of time, Jonas was a landlord in Chicago, and when he first started, he knew nothing about how to fix anything. Over time, he got frustrated by having to call someone for help anytime anything broke, so he taught himself more and more basic repair skills. But in the beginning, he was useless at maintenance, much to the frustration (we're sure!) of the good folks who lived downstairs in his three-flat (Chicago-speak for a three-unit building). He was incredibly jealous of others he knew who could handle most fixes when a renter called. That usually made for a much better experience for all involved.

They may understand the importance of property upkeep, or they may not. One of the biggest mistakes that individual landlords often make is to ignore maintenance items. Just like we mentioned for homeowners, there are regular items that need to be maintained, like siding, plumbing, roofs, etc. Oftentimes, to save money, individual landlords patch things instead of replacing them. Sometimes, they may not even know what needs to be done. Some can get away with this for a long time, even though the reality is that a well-maintained property performs better for the landlord in the long run. But, again, these individual landlords aren't always professional landlords. They're often balancing being landlords with working their day jobs and tending to their other responsibilities, so fixing things that may seem optional to them can take a backseat—even though those things may seem far more important to you.

The most important thing for you to remember with this type of landlord is that they're someone a lot like you. They're trying to balance a complicated life, and managing your home is one piece of their puzzle.

If you can be understanding and helpful toward them, they'll likely be understanding and helpful toward you. If you're friendly and respectful with them, they'll likely be friendly and respectful with you.

Of course, this is not always the case—your landlord might be mean or disrespectful, and because they're an individual landlord, there's not necessarily a higher authority you can go to in order to report them (unless they behave illegally). If your landlord doesn't treat you with the kindness and respect you deserve, you might feel that you have to put up with it because they own your rental property, and that's an awful situation. If you have an individual landlord, it's worth doing what you can to make sure you get along with them on a personal level to avoid conflicts like these.

LANDLORD TYPE #2: CORPORATE OWNER/OPERATORS

These companies are, in many ways, a lot like individual landlords but bigger—sometimes much, much bigger. The biggest and best-known companies in this group have names like Equity Residential, found across the country; Essex Property Trust, found all over the West Coast; the Irvine Company, found in California; and Edward Rose, found in the Midwest. There are many firms like these operating in nearly every city.

Like individual landlords, they own and operate their properties, and they have full responsibility for every aspect of the property and the ability to make all their own decisions about how to manage each property.

Their size, however, can make them very different in how they operate.

On the plus side, they can be very well organized and very professional. They care deeply about their reputation and often do a great job of providing you, their customer, with great customer service. Want super-fast maintenance services, sometimes within a couple of hours? Want someone to receive your packages for you? This is usually the type of landlord that's set up to provide those kinds of services.

Their large size can also allow them to get you access to benefits and amenities that might not be available at smaller properties or with smaller landlords. Moving concierges, apps for submitting maintenance requests, discounts at local businesses, and free yoga classes are just a few examples of things we've seen from these companies.

These companies are usually the best positioned to take great care of their properties, which means you get a well-maintained home for as long as you're living there. Their employees are experienced professionals, for one, so they'll have certain protocols in place to keep things running smoothly. Additionally, these companies have the resources to take care of any maintenance issues that may come up during your stay in your rental. Many individual landlords can't make such a guarantee, as we've discussed. And, unlike the next group we will discuss—the third-party property managers—they have full control of the property because they both own and manage it.

There are drawbacks, however. Depending on the company and the local manager, they can be quite rigid and inflexible. They often have firm rules set by the owner or the company, and the person you're dealing with is doing what they have to in terms of implementing those rules. But we all know that your home is a very personal place to you, and you may need a little grace for any number of reasons. In some of these properties, however, the rules are the rules, and you may get less flexibility than you might prefer.

This may mean getting parking tickets with lightning speed when your guest parks in the wrong spot or getting an eviction notice on your door (ack!) because you forgot to update your automatic rent payment and the rent was a day late.

They're also pretty aggressive about keeping rent at "market" levels, which means you can count on paying full price for these apartments when you move in, and when you stay or renew your lease, there's rarely any deals to be had from these landlords.

LANDLORD TYPE #3: THIRD-PARTY PROPERTY MANAGERS

This group of landlords, the second-largest group, is probably the most misunderstood of all.

These folks manage properties for property owners. If a landlord owns a property and decides they can't manage it on their own, they hire one of these property-management companies. That's why it's called third-party management. They're not the occupant or an individual managing a home that they own; they're not the owner/operator; they're a third group involved in the property.

These companies can be enormous businesses. The largest landlord in the United States is a company called Greystar, which is (mostly) a third-party property-management company. As of 2022, it managed about 700,000 apartments, which is almost one out of every fifty in the country.

Most third-party property-management companies aren't like that, though. Most of them are dramatically smaller—usually just a handful of people running a couple hundred or a few thousand properties.

What's important for you to understand is that because these groups don't own the properties themselves, third-party property managers have very different incentives than property owners do.

Those incentives are tied up in the way they get paid by the owner. Usually, property managers get paid a percentage of the property's revenues (mostly rent); plus, they get to recover the expenses they incur in managing the property—salaries for the staff working there, maintenance costs, etc.

This leads to some subtle but important differences between owners/operators and third-party property managers.

The biggest difference is that it's not the third-party property manager's money behind the property—it's the property owner's money. So when something needs to be fixed or upgraded, the manager needs to get someone else's permission. They can't just act alone and make their own decisions about what to upgrade or fix.

Usually, with routine maintenance, there's no issues with this. The owners usually give them the authority and budget to take care of day-to-day fixes. But with some owners and with bigger investments and repairs, this could mean delays or decisions not to do things that seem logical to everyone who's there at the property in person.

When this happens, it's one of the bigger sources of frustration for both property managers and residents. The property manager knows something should be done. You, the resident, know something should be done. But, for whatever reason, the owner isn't willing to allow the property manager to do the work. As a result, the property manager gets squeezed into a difficult situation trying to balance the needs of their two customers—those living in the property and the owners who hired them to manage the property.

Another way to think about third-party property managers is how they get paid. With an owner/operator or individual landlord, they get all the rent minus the property expenses. The third-party property manager generally just gets paid a small slice of the rent (usually 2–7 percent), so their primary incentive is really just to keep the owner happy and to hold on to the account.

For most property managers, this incentive structure doesn't make much difference in how they work. They're good folks trying their best to do a good job like the rest of us. But, unfortunately, in some cases, this difference can lead to some strange decision-making where the third-party manager ends up doing as little as possible at the property so their fees are as profitable for them as possible.

To the owner, sometimes these property managers look great in the short term because, by doing less, these property managers might spend less of the owners' money, leading to more profits. In the long term, however, this almost always ends badly for all involved. The property ends up needing a lot of expensive catch-up maintenance. You, the resident, end up living through both the pain of maintenance not getting done and then extreme maintenance events (sewage backup, anyone? Ew!) occurring, and the owner ends up footing the bill.

Again, this isn't the case for most third-party property managers. Most are great at their jobs and work hard to make both renters and owners happy, but it can be tough for them to get that right every time, given the nature of their business model.

THE LANDLORD'S TEAM MEMBERS

So, who will you encounter in each of these landlord situations? So much of your experience in your place will come down to who you're actually dealing with most of the time, so let's talk about the types of roles associated with these types of landlords.

Individual Landlord

Individual landlords are the owners and the operators. The most important thing to know about working with them is that it's their place, and the buck stops with them.

Their biggest challenge? This isn't usually their day job. For them, this is an evenings and weekends kind of thing, if they even live in the same area. So it can be a challenge to get in contact with them and get the service you're hoping for.

Leasing Agents and Brokers

Leasing agents and brokers are the folks at corporate owner/operators or third-party property managers who rent you your apartment or house. They're the first people you meet, and they're the salespeople representing the owner/operator/property manager. They should know a lot about the place and what it's like to live there. Remember, it's their job to make the place sound great and to get you to sign a lease. After you move in, they might help you with packages or to get maintenance issues reported.

Their biggest challenge? This role tends to suffer from high turnover, so these folks are usually relatively new to the community and the profession and don't always have all the information you might want them to have.

Maintenance Staff

Maintenance staff fix the issues that arise in your place. Water leaking? Heater not working? Toilet backed up? These are the ones who will turn up when you yelp for help, and bigger owners/operators and property managers have a full-time team of maintenance folks to take care of their properties.

They have to deal with a ton of different types of issues and work hard to take great care of the residents they work with. They're often residents' favorite people at an apartment community. After all, who doesn't love a person who can fix the thing that's driving you nuts?

Their biggest challenge? They get pulled in a hundred different directions—sometimes literally. Jonas has seen maintenance-team members go out in the morning with eight service requests to handle (each one a unique resident's problem) only to return in the evening having taken care of ten requests but none of the original eight they had in the morning because all day long emergencies kept coming up.

Superintendent/Resident Manager/Building Manager

In smaller communities, there are sometimes folks who operate on behalf of the owner or property manager as a kind of part-time property manager and maintenance person. They try to do it all—and do so, usually while holding down another job, because the pay they get for this role is discounted or free rent.

Their biggest challenge? These jobs are nearly impossible to do well. The best work from home so they're at the property most of the time, but, even still, they have other responsibilities. Try to be patient with them.

Tradespeople and Vendors

Regardless of the size of your rental or the type of landlord, sooner or later, there are tradespeople who will show up when the work that needs to get done exceeds the skills or workload of the team at the property. They could be plumbers, electricians, carpenters, landscapers, or other professionals.

Their biggest challenge? They have no relationship with you, the renter. Their relationship is entirely with the landlord, so they can struggle to interact effectively with renters.

Community Managers, Assistant Managers, and Regional Managers

These are the folks who have overall responsibility for a community or group of communities. They're the management. Depending on the nature of your community, you may see these folks a lot or not at all.

Their biggest challenge? They're managing a huge range of responsibilities, almost always with far too few resources and far too few team members. As a result, they're usually very stretched and trying to figure out how to get everything done with less.

We know we just threw a ton of information at you, but remember that you can refer back to this section whenever you get lost or confused. As you navigate the rental process, these different types of companies and people will become more familiar, so don't worry if you feel overwhelmed at this point.

> **Remember:** Understanding your landlord's perspective can help you with everything from finding the right place to making the most of your home.

1.3

THE LANDLORD–RENTER POWER DYNAMIC

Landlord–tenant relationships take many different forms. Some are friendly, characterized by kindness and warmth. Some are combative, full of arguments and frustrations. Many relationships land somewhere in the middle as professional and courteous—nothing more, nothing less. After all, the agreement you entered into with your landlord is a business transaction, and it should be centered on reciprocation and mutual interest.

These relationships often shift over time, too, as your life within your rental goes through its ups and downs. You may have started off liking your landlord, but maybe things have soured since the start of your tenancy. Perhaps your landlord was iffy about you at the beginning but has since warmed up to you. These emotional shifts in your relationship can have high stakes because there is a certain power imbalance between you as a renter and your landlord. The fact is that this person owns your home. The property you live in isn't your property. Your landlord controls whether you're allowed to stay in your home and how much money you'll pay to do so. This is true no matter how good or bad your relationship with your landlord is.

Knowing that someone could potentially unhouse you or even simply make maintenance decisions that differ from what you would prefer can make it hard for you to advocate for yourself. If your landlord is unfair or threatening, you might feel that you have to put up with it because of the power they hold over your housing situation. This is especially true if you're low-income or part of other marginalized groups, such as if you're living with a disability, are a person of color, or are LGBTQIA+. You might feel that your choices for safe, affordable housing are few and far between. It's understandable that you'd feel scared, upset, and even angry about a tumultuous relationship with your landlord.

Thankfully, our country has begun to talk more and more about the landlord–tenant relationship. During the COVID-19 pandemic and its aftereffects, the housing crisis in our country reached a boiling point. We saw a rise in discourse around renting, tenants, and landlords. There was a surge in the development of tenants' rights groups, mutual-aid networks, and other groups ensuring that tenants were housed even if they couldn't pay their rent. The eviction moratorium helped people, too, although the moratorium is over now. Our interest in renter advocacy doesn't have to be over, though. We can keep pushing these discussions forward, talking about how to make renting as safe and sustainable as possible.

We want renting to be as equitable as possible. This means that we've got to face up to the difficulties of being a renter and help you through them. So how exactly do you advocate for yourself when dealing with someone who owns your home? Let's talk about some of your best strategies.

KNOW YOUR RIGHTS

One of the biggest ways you can advocate for yourself as a tenant is to understand your legal rights before you even sign a lease. Some of these rights are federal, like your right not to face discrimination in the housing process or your right to live in habitable conditions. Of course, such rights will apply no matter where you live in America.

Some of these rights, however, will be specific to your state or area. Look for resources online that break down your local laws (tenants' rights groups will often provide such materials). Get familiar with the websites of your local housing authorities and the numbers of any landlord-complaint lines.

If you know your rights, you'll be able to understand if you're not being treated in accordance with the law, and you can take action. Knowledge is power.

COMMUNICATE WITH OTHER RENTERS

If you're having an issue with your rental and your landlord won't act on it, one way to work toward change is to talk to the other renters around you. To do this, some form associations or unions in order to have a place to discuss their grievances and decide how to take action together. These associations can involve people who share a building, a neighborhood, a landlord, a property manager, or something else.

If you want to join a renters' association, it's important to understand how the law treats organizing. Currently, there is no national precedent that protects tenant organizing, so it all comes down to where you live. Depending on your place of residence, your right to organize as a tenant may or may not be specifically enumerated in your state or local laws—in New York, for example, this right is specified.

In most cases, even if that specific right is not on the books, there are laws protecting tenants from retaliation when they do decide to organize, often for some explicit period of time (six months is common). Doing your own research will help you understand exactly how you are protected by the law if you choose to form or join a tenants' association or union. Your landlord does not have to recognize your tenants' association, but that does not mean you cannot be part of it. It's your decision to make.

Of course, you don't have to join an association or union. These organizations are most popular in New York City and other urban centers where there are lots of people living in the same building or who have the same landlord. Most individual landlords only have one or two tenants, however, so maybe there aren't enough people around you to form a group. Whatever your circumstances, discussing your grievances with other tenants can be a powerful tool. Banding together with renters in similar situations will bring comfort and sympathy, and it will also make the impact of your advocacy stronger. It may be easy to ignore one person's complaint, but your landlord will find it harder to ignore several complaints.

Say, for example, it's the middle of winter, and the hot water in your building has been out for a week. Your landlord knows but hasn't done anything about it. You could get together with other renters in your building and write a letter to your landlord, explaining that you're going to withhold rent until the hot-water issue is resolved. (In most states, you would have the legal right to withhold rent in circumstances like this.) That would probably spur your landlord to act more quickly.

Renters' associations can make it easier for renters to talk amongst themselves in this way and decide what to do, but you can take action with your neighbors in whatever way you think is best.

RECOGNIZE YOUR OWN POWER

You may think that your landlord has all of the power in your relationship, but you have power, too. As we've discussed, you are empowered through your tenants' rights organizations and federal, state, and local laws. You also have collective power when you come together with other tenants.

On top of that, your rent provides your landlord's income, or part of it. Without you, your landlord's rental unit would be empty, and your landlord would be without that source of income. You are the reason that the unit is profitable, and that's powerful, too. You are your landlord's customer, and that means you should expect them to treat you like the important customer you are.

It's important to understand your landlord's needs when you're navigating your relationship with them. You want to understand what they're concerned about, like the financial drain of a vacant rental, or a pet ruining their units, or a tenant refusing to pay rent. When you understand what makes them behave the way they do, you'll be a more effective negotiator on your own behalf. Understand what your landlord needs and what you can give them. Understand what you need and what your landlord can give you.

TREAT YOUR LANDLORD AS A PERSON

When we're angry or upset, we often think of the person we're mad at as a monster. It's not true, though. Keep this in mind as you go forward: your landlord is a human being, just like you. No matter how frustrating you find them, and no matter how angry you are, it's an important thing to remember. Human beings can treat each other unfairly, of course. Human beings can be upsetting and frustrating, and they can make each other angry. This is especially true when one of them has a certain power over the other, like your landlord, who, literally and figuratively, holds the key to your housing.

But treating someone with respect and courtesy can go further than you might think. Even if things get heated, you can make the choice to bring things back around to calm decency. Your landlord may appreciate it enough to make negotiations smoother.

1.4

HOW LANDLORDS MAKE MONEY

Making money is a big part of what drives landlords, so understanding how they make money will help you understand the choices they make.

Their profit starts with the rent, but it's not all about the rent.

The rent they receive from you is the overwhelming majority of the revenue or income they receive from their properties, but it's not the real way they make money.

Huh? The rent isn't how the landlord makes money? We know, that seems counterintuitive.

The reason is that the rent is *assumed*. The landlord has mostly fixed costs and fixed revenues, so the monthly rent they get from you is critical, but it's what happens around the rent that determines whether the property is really profitable for the landlord.

In order to make money, the landlord's revenue (again, mostly rent) needs to be more than the landlord's costs, which are things like mortgage payments, taxes, insurance, maintenance, payroll/benefits, and utilities.

Landlords maximize their income by taking every available opportunity to improve revenue by lowering costs, but they have very few ways they can do that. Let's go over the major ways.

1. **Avoid vacancy.**
   An empty rental is one that generates no rent at all. This is one of the most expensive costs for landlords, and smart landlords try to minimize the time that their places sit empty. A month of vacancy is the same as an 8 percent reduction in a year's rent to the landlord.

   As a result, most landlords would like you to move in sooner or have you stay in your place so they can avoid vacancy.

2. **Avoid turnover.**
   Turnover is when an existing renter moves out and a new one moves in. This creates the potential for vacancy between rentals, and on top of that, new renters also (reasonably) expect the place to be in great shape.

   At minimum, that means cleaning up most or all signs of the old resident, often requiring new paint, new carpet, and repairs to appliances and any other minor matters. This cost (called a "turn" by industry folks) can run into the thousands of dollars and is usually avoided when a resident stays in the place and renews the lease.

   Again, landlords hate vacancy and the costs of turnover, so they want you to stay.

3. **Charge market rent.**
   Most of us think of landlords as setting the rent, but that's not exactly true. Landlords actually have very limited power to set the rent.

   Here's why: if a landlord decides to raise the rent, but you know you could rent other similar places for less, you are very likely to move to one of those other places. In that case, the landlord would have to deal with vacancy and turnover, both

of which have a bigger impact on the landlord's profits than maximizing the rent would.

So landlords make sure they're charging market rent each year and that you, their renter, are paying a similar price for the place as you would pay for similar places nearby.

As with most prices, market rent rises each year, and most landlords will make small increases each year to ensure they stay at or close to the market price as best as they can.

4. **Be smart about maintenance and expenses.**
There are some landlords out there who think that they should avoid every maintenance expense, and there are some out there who simply can't afford to do proper maintenance. In the long run, however, these are expensive and unproductive approaches.

Poor maintenance leads to unhappy residents, which means higher turnover, lower rent, and unplanned maintenance, which is almost always more expensive than planned, well-timed maintenance. So, while most landlords are not seeking to minimize their expenses, they are thinking strategically about the maintenance they choose to perform and when.

5. **Avoid difficult renters.**
Most renters are good folks who just want to live peacefully in their homes, so the overwhelming majority of us are no problem for landlords.

Sadly, there are some bad apples out there who can be brutal, and most landlords have heard enough horror stories from their friends to be afraid of these folks.

When a renter goes bad on a landlord, it can be horribly stressful and expensive. A single bad renter can cause tens of thousands of dollars of damage to a place and can cause months or even years of vacancy, legal fees, or unpaid rent. These renters have been known to put landlords into real financial trouble, even causing bankruptcy.

Whatever you may think of your landlord or landlords in general, this is important to understanding their psychology.

For some landlords, avoiding this risk is their biggest driver, and they will do almost anything to avoid someone who might cause this kind of situation for them.

6. **Sell a property to get the appreciation.**
   It can take a long time or a short time, depending on what happens in the market, but over time, rental properties usually get more valuable. As a result, one way that landlords make profits from their properties is to sell them. This actually happens less often than you would think, and many landlords sit on profits for a long, long time.

   Why? There are big tax incentives for landlords to hold on to properties. It's a very weird thing for our government to choose to do—to create an incentive for landlords to hold on to rental properties for a long time—but that's what we have.

   What does the sale of your rental mean for you? Well, that's a longer answer. Check out Section 4.12 for all the details.

DO LANDLORDS MAKE A LOT OF MONEY?

It depends. Individual landlords are usually affluent individuals who become landlords as a result of having some extra money available to them or by inheriting a property.

Companies that own real estate aren't known for being particularly profitable, but they are very dependable and low-risk sources of investment profits for those who own them.

Strange to think about it, but the properties themselves, particularly in the early years, often make very little money for the landlord.

The landlord has to pay for their mortgage, insurance, maintenance, leasing fees, and more. And, often, those expenses add up to the full monthly amount of the rent being paid.

That said, much of the mortgage expense goes to paying down the mortgage. While the landlord may be "cash flow negative" (more cash going out than coming in) at times, some of the cash that they have to pay is reducing the debt they owe on the mortgage, so they are building up an asset.

As a result, some landlords can be pretty strapped for cash and can struggle to keep up with all the expenses of a property. But when it comes time to sell the property or when the mortgage is paid off or refinanced, they can come into quite a bit of money.

WHAT DOES THIS ALL MEAN FOR YOU?

First, because you now know that the most important way a landlord makes money is by keeping their place occupied, you can use that to your advantage.

Your landlord has real costs to pay if you move out, so you can see the value they place on keeping you in the rental and understand that they might be willing to trade something for that. This is particularly true for small landlords because they don't have a big portfolio of properties to spread vacancy losses across. If the landlord only has one or two places (as is the case with most individual landlords), then vacancy is the difference between some income and no income.

Second, understand that your rent is going to go up pretty much every year. It's not pleasant to have your cost of living go up each year, but now it won't be a surprise. How much? More of that is up to you than you may think. Check out Section 2.10 to learn more about negotiating when it comes to renewing your lease.

Third, help your landlord maintain your apartment. How? By reporting issues right away and making your place available when they need to send over a contractor, plumber, electrician, or other type of maintenance professional. It's always an inconvenience to have maintenance folks in your place, but the fact that your landlord is sending them over is almost always a sign of a good landlord trying to do the right thing to manage your property and make it great for you. We talk more about maintenance in Section 4.7.

Finally, do your part as a tenant. What does this look like in practice? Be as polite as you would expect your landlord to be to you, and respond to your landlord's communications as clearly and promptly as possible (as you would want them to respond to you). You'll want to be especially careful to communicate when you're going to be late on a payment or when you're unable to do something your landlord has asked of you. Take care of the rental property as best you can—it's your home and the landlord's property. Stick to the rules of the lease. Your landlord is going to be much more likely to give you a deal on that upcoming lease renewal if they like you!

Keep in mind, however, that being a good tenant doesn't mean you have to let your landlord mistreat you. Quite the opposite: if you're being treated unfairly or illegally, you should absolutely advocate for yourself. (We'll discuss some tools for that later on in other sections, like when we cover housing discrimination and eviction in Sections 1.9 and 4.13, respectively.) Some people want so badly to avoid conflict with their landlords that they struggle to stand up for themselves. Instead, they end up miserable. This is not what we mean when we talk about being a good tenant. Instead, we mean that your landlord is likely to treat you with kindness and respect if you treat them with the same.

Remember: If you understand what drives your landlord financially, you can understand why they make the decisions they do, and that will give you an advantage.

1.5

RENTAL FRAUD AND HOW TO AVOID GETTING SCAMMED

To say fraud is widespread in rentals is a little like saying that Tom Brady is a pretty good football player or that Lady Gaga has some talent.

Sadly, fraud is everywhere in rentals. In part, that's why we started Dwellsy—to create a fraud-free space for renters and landlords.

Renting a home or apartment is already stressful without having to worry about getting scammed. Going through hundreds of listings, contacting landlords, haggling for lower rent, finding a place that will take your dog, and working out the utility expenses—shouldn't that be enough?

A Dwellsy survey in 2022 showed that 44 percent of renters experience a fraud loss in the rental search or have a close friend or family member who has experienced a fraud loss in the rental search.

The average renter with a loss to these terrible fraudsters loses $2,890, which, to most Americans, is a substantial part of their savings. Some are conned out of even more. This kind of loss is brutal and crushing, and it can take years to recover from it.

We're not going to let this happen to you. Let's start by understanding what rental fraud looks like and how it works.

TYPES OF RENTAL FRAUD

There are two basic types of fraud that affect renters.

The first, and most common, we call the "fake-landlord scam." In this scenario, a fraudster poses as a landlord, often stealing a real listing from a legitimate site and reposting it on the same or a different listing site with the intent of directly defrauding renters.

In most cases, all that has changed from the original listing is the rent price and the contact information for the landlord or listing agent. Usually, the price is now *very* attractive, and instead of the legitimate representative of the property, now it's the scammer's contact information. In some cases, these scams modify a sale listing instead of a rental listing, as the two often look the same in many ways.

With this scam, the scammer posts the fraudulent listing and waits for a renter to contact them. When an unsuspecting and hopeful renter does reach out and inquire about the listing, the scammer works hard to seem just like any other landlord (though perhaps a little more responsive) and may run the renter through a seemingly normal rental process—with a few quirks, like making it difficult or impossible to see the actual place. They might even run an application process, capturing social security numbers and other confidential information in the process—ack!

Once the renter sends the deposit, typically first and last month's rent and/or a security deposit, the scammer disappears, never to be heard from again, unless they subsequently engage in identity theft, which creates a whole secondary nightmare.

For renters, this scam is the primary threat. And it's an enormous danger. For most people, first and last month's rent is thousands of dollars, and in many cases, it's all of the money they have in savings.

Recall that in our survey we learned the average loss was enormous—nearly $3,000. But the real impact to a renter searching for a place is even worse than the money lost. Imagine yourself in this situation:

> *You think you've found your dream place. Sure, the landlord seems a little squirrelly, but aren't they all? You can afford the place, they'll take your cat, they're okay with your credit being less than perfect, and they didn't even ask for a guarantor! And the rent is even less than you were hoping to pay, which means you'll be able to save a few bucks each month and maybe afford the occasional holiday. Who says you can't have it all?*
>
> *With some friends, you pack up your stuff in a rented truck and head over to the new place. But wait . . . the landlord who said he would be there to meet you is nowhere to be found.*
>
> *Worse, there's a very, very confused person who's there already, living in the apartment. And she seems to think she lives there. She knows nothing about you or your lease. She calls her landlord, who also knows nothing about your lease. You show her the lease you signed, frantically texting your landlord, who, all of a sudden, is unresponsive, leaving you sitting on a curb, all of your worldly belongings in a truck, with nowhere to live and nowhere to go.*

Let's make sure this never happens to you. More in a moment about how to avoid this scam.

The second type of rental scam, the "fake-renter scam," is the opposite of the first type. With this one, the scammer positions themself as a renter inquiring to a landlord about a rental.

The usual approach is to offer to pay for a full year's rent up front, and the fraudster then runs into fake "troubles" that require a short-term loan from the landlord in order to make the troubles go away. The landlord, hoping for the full year of rent paid up front, advances the loan—only to have the fraudster disappear.

While in most cases this won't affect renters like you directly, it is good to know about because most landlords now receive fake inquiries from scammers like this, and it's made them suspicious of renters who seem too good to be true in one way or another.

HOW DID IT GET THIS BAD?

We can't quite pin the whole fraud problem on Craigslist, but, well . . . let's go back a few years.

Until 2015 or so, for most of the United States, Craigslist was the main way you found a rental in most cities (except NYC, but that's another story). Kludgy as it was, people bought and sold everything on it, and that included housing. Craigslist was chock-full of renters and landlords during its golden era.

There are a few factors that we think created a perfect circumstance for the emergence of a massive rental-fraud problem.

1. **Anonymity.** Both renters and landlords are completely anonymous on Craigslist, so neither has any idea who they're dealing with.
2. **Large, urgent transactions.** There is a lot of money changing hands between strangers in a rental transaction, and there's often real urgency around the deal.
3. **Rise of irreversible payments.** Venmo, Zelle, and other irreversible payment tools are now widely used.

So, let's dig into these three, because understanding them and why they're dangerous is critical to keeping you safe.

Anonymity = Risk

Anonymity is one of the cornerstones of the "old internet"; anonymity ruled almost everywhere. It used to be that you could be anyone you wanted to be online.

Unfortunately, that gave rise to a lot of bad behavior, and one of the original innovations that changed the internet and made it far safer and far more accessible was the transition to dealing in real names. With the rise of Facebook, LinkedIn, and Google accounts, your online profiles quickly became attached to who you were in real life because they demanded that you use your real first and last names in order to find other people. By interacting with real people, you could trust others to be accountable for their actions—and be held accountable for your own.

If you're a fraudster in the world of real names, you need an oasis, a place where you can transact anonymously, and Craigslist was and still is that place. It's a place where no one knows who you are and you can act with impunity.

Big Dollars and Real Urgency

Like everyone else, fraudsters go where the biggest opportunities are. And rent fraud is a big opportunity.

For most of us, rent is our biggest expense each month, and putting down first and last month's rent or a security deposit is often the biggest check that renters ever cut—thousands of dollars in many cases.

Add to that the fact that there is urgency around securing your new place ("Put your deposit down now; it might be gone tomorrow!"), and lots of renters are forced to throw caution to the wind and trust someone that they might not ordinarily trust.

Combine lots of money changing hands, real urgency, a heightened need to take a risk, and an anonymous platform, and what do you get? Fraud paradise!

Venmo and Zelle Are One-Way Roads

We're all used to using tools like Venmo and Zelle to send money between friends and family—that's what they were designed to do.

Increasingly, though, they're being used to pay businesses for services received. Most of the time, that goes just fine. But we've all heard horror stories of payments gone wrong.

If we're lucky, the recipient is well meaning and sends the money back. But what if that recipient is an intentional fraudster who was out to steal from you? Then the money is just gone. The terms and conditions outlined by Venmo and Zelle are very clear on that point. They will not help you get your money back. They're very different than other payment platforms in that regard.

Together, these three points have combined to create a nightmare for thousands of renters—more than 20 percent of us. Stick to the following ten steps to make sure fraud doesn't happen to you.

DWELLSY'S TEN STEPS TO STAY SAFE IN THE RENTAL SEARCH

So what's a renter to do? Follow these steps to stay safe in your search.

1. Use Reputable Sources for Rental Listings

A safe search starts with staying away from anonymous sites like Craigslist or unknown, unbranded rental-listing sites. Just don't use them—the risk is far too great.

There are highly reputable sites out there that do a very good job of keeping the fraudsters at bay using two different approaches.

The old-fashioned way of doing this is to charge apartment managers to list properties. The upside of this approach is that few fraudsters are willing to pay to list, so these sites, like Apartments.com and Apartment List, are pretty safe as a result. The downside is that relatively few landlords are willing to pay to list their places, so the inventory of these sites is limited to the few landlords who are willing and able to pay for listings—mostly those who own larger apartment communities.

At Dwellsy, we have a different approach, which is to build a marketplace with zero fraud as the goal from the beginning. In part, we do this by using an identity and address verification system staffed by real humans.

We could go on about how we fight fraud for hours, but that's not what this book is about. Suffice it to say that we believe we're the safest rental marketplace, and we wake up every day and work toward Fraud Zero.

While Dwellsy may be the safest place to search, there are others that are relatively safe. Here's a list of the rental sites that we consider amongst the safest and most reputable:

ApartmentGuide (Redfin)
Apartment List
Apartments.com (CoStar)
Dwellsy
ForRent.com (CoStar)
HotPads (Zillow)
Redfin
Rent.com (Redfin)
StreetEasy (Zillow)
Trulia (Zillow)
Zillow
Zumper

Note that in many cases, these sites are owned by the same big companies—such as Zillow, CoStar, and Redfin—so they may have the same rentals across multiple sites, though the user experience may be different in each one. (We've tried to identify where that's the case above so that you don't waste your time.) Regardless, all of these sites (except Dwellsy) operate on a buyer-beware basis, so you still need to be very, very careful.

What does "buyer-beware" mean? Buyer-beware means it's your responsibility to keep yourself safe, and the platform takes no responsibility for keeping you safe. Dwellsy is the only platform that offers the SafeSearch guarantee. With the others, you're on your own, so make sure you take extra precautions.

Using a SafeSearch site is a great start, but read on for other precautions to take.

2. Check the Landlord's Online Credentials

Landlords are people, too. Unless they're businesses. And like any other person or business, they should have a normal online presence.

If your potential landlord is an individual (which is the case for most US rentals), then they should show up like a real person on the internet. Do they have a LinkedIn profile? A Facebook page? An Instagram account?

Not that you want to get creepy or stalker-ish, but you should be able to easily establish that they have a normal online presence like anyone else you may search for.

If your prospective landlord is a company, then they should have a website. Let's be honest, many property-management companies have lousy websites, but they should still have one. Also, such a company is often a member of a local trade association (so you may be able to find it listed on the association's website), or it may have a social-media presence.

Do you know who doesn't have a normal online presence? A scammer. Usually, a scammer has no online presence at all, or the one they have is odd. If you're dealing with a landlord, they should have an online presence that makes sense for who they are.

3. See the Place—the Inside of the Place

Perhaps the most conspicuous of all tactics scammers use in renting scams is not letting the renter see the property before signing the lease.

Don't let anyone convince you to go without checking the inside of the property before closing the deal. No matter how sincere the person you're talking to seems, you should know that viewing the unit in person is your right, and you shouldn't give up that right under any circumstances. Remain persistent and make sure that you inspect your potential home or apartment before signing a lease or handing over any personal information or money.

If you're in town and can take the time to visit the place in person, then stop by and take a tour. That's the easiest way to get this done. But—and this is important—make sure you tour the *inside*. Seeing the outside isn't enough.

If you're out of town, you can still "see" the place. How?

- Get a live video tour from the agent or owner from their phone. They can use a live video-chat tool like Zoom, FaceTime, or Google Meet to show you the place.
- Get a friend or family member to visit the place for you.
- Plan a weekend or one-day visit, if you can swing it.

Regardless, make sure the place matches the photos you've seen, inside and out.

4. Meet the Landlord or Their Representative

For every rental, there's a human behind it. And you get to meet the human. No excuses.

One of the most common features of rental fraud is the ever-absent landlord. If the person you're in contact with about a rental tells you they're out of town or that they're too busy to meet you in person and can't even do a video call or a phone call, alarms should go off in your mind immediately.

In particular, if they will only talk to you via text message, that's a very large red flag. That's what scammers do.

5. Take Your Time Before Sending Money

In rental-listing scams, scammers often ask renters to send money very quickly.

Real landlords don't generally apply much, if any, pressure to close the deal. Real landlords usually have lots of renters like you interested in their place. They may let you know that if you don't take action, you'll lose the place, but they rarely use hardball tactics to close the deal.

If you feel like the landlord is applying a significant amount of pressure on you to close the deal, then, more than likely, it's not a legitimate deal. Even if it is a legitimate deal, then it's likely you're overpaying because landlords usually have lots of choices for who to rent to.

Either way, tell the landlord (fake or otherwise) that you need some time to decide, and see what happens. Slow down and take your time when you're worried. It's better to lose out on a potential rental than to lose thousands of dollars to a thief.

6. Don't Believe in Discounts or Free Lunches

Another common fraudster tactic to get quick payment of first and last month's rent or a security deposit is to offer steep discounts of 20 percent or more on the up-front payments or the ongoing rent.

Because the scammer knows you're never going to move into the place and that they're not going to collect rent on an ongoing basis, they won't lose a dime by lowering the rent. And if they can create urgency and close the scam faster for 20 percent less, that's still well worth their time.

Real landlords rarely, if ever, discount the rent, and when they do, it's as a result of you negotiating it (yes, you can negotiate the rent—check out Section 2.10 for more information about how to do so). They might give you a discounted security deposit, and they might be running a move-in special that gives you a few weeks of free rent. That can happen, particularly with larger communities, but those deals actually reduce the amount of money the landlord gets up front.

A real landlord will *never* give you a big discount off the monthly rent to get you to pay right now. But a fraudster will.

7. Watch Out for Rent That's Too Good to Be True

There are deals out there, so it can be difficult to determine those that are real and those that are too good to be true.

There's a concept called "market rent"—that's essentially the "right" price for a rental. Renters who are in the market for a rental usually have the best sense of this. If you're looking for a one-bedroom in a particular area, and you've looked at a hundred different places, you know exactly which ones are priced about right (at market rent), which ones are overpriced (above market rent), and which ones are underpriced (below market rent).

You know who's lousy at setting the right price for rentals? Landlords. The reality for them is that they just don't have as much information about pricing as renters do, so they often get it wrong.

Some landlords underprice a property and, lucky you, you get a deal. Usually, the landlord figures it out over time, and you'll be looking at some heftier rent increases later on, but in the beginning, you get to enjoy the lower rent.

Other landlords have an intentional strategy of renting at below market rent because they know that when they do this, it tends to attract renters who'll stay a long time.

So, there *are* deals out there.

But how do you know when the deal is too good to be true? Well, look closely and see how far from the market price the rent is.

- Beachfront California luxury condo for $700/month that should rent for $4,000/month? Scam for sure.
- Studio apartment in Omaha for $2,500 a month that should rent for $1,000/month? Almost definitely a scam.
- One-bedroom apartment in Cincinnati for $700/month that should rent for $850/month? Potentially legit.
- Two-bedroom apartment in Atlanta for $1,850/month that should rent for $1,700/month? Likely legit.

There's no hard-and-fast rule of thumb, but in general, if the price is within 20 percent of what you think it should be, then it is likely just the landlord getting the rent wrong. If it's more than 20 percent off, then it's likely a sign of a scam.

8. Beware of Those Who Ask for Personal Information

One common way that scammers steal a little extra money is through identity theft, and the rental application process is rife with opportunities for accessing your personal information.

The process most legitimate landlords follow will require you to provide sensitive information, including your social security number, your driver's license information, your income information, and other juicy stuff that you might not even give your mother if she asked.

This is one of those rare occasions when this type of information is genuinely needed, and scammers know that you're expecting landlords to ask for this info. This creates a weak point in the process for you, and the scammer knows how valuable this info is to them, so they're quick to ask for it right up front. Even if they aren't successful in scamming you out of rent money or a security deposit, at least this way they can steal your identity. Ouch.

So beware of anyone asking for this kind of personal information, particularly early in the process. When they do ask for the information, make sure they have a very professional process for you to enter it, preferably a secure online application system.

9. Be Careful with Apps Like PayPal, Venmo, and Zelle

It used to be that rent was paid by check, which made things much more difficult for scammers. Now, PayPal, Venmo, Zelle, and similar methods are commonplace, and we're all used to using them—including, maybe, your next landlord. Paying your rent by Venmo sounds great, right? Super convenient! Yes, but . . .

Venmo, Zelle, and similar tools are great right up until you realize that they are one-way payment tools with no ability to reverse charges in the event that fraud is discovered.

Fraudulent transaction on your credit card? Contact the card company and report it. They'll reverse the charge. Wrote a check and changed your mind? Contact the bank and issue a stop payment.

It doesn't work like that with Venmo or Zelle. The payment is issued immediately and, once issued, cannot be recovered, except with the cooperation of the person who received your money. Your friend who you paid $100 instead of $10 for your share of the drinks bill? No problem—she'll Venmo you back. The scammer who stole $5,000 from you? You'll never hear from them again.

Make sure you are certain the transaction is completely legitimate before using one of these tools to pay a new landlord. There are no second chances and no backsies available to you.

Even though you may want to use these tools when you've moved in, it can be a prudent choice to make your initial payments to the landlord through some of the old-fashioned methods—check or credit card. Just keep in mind that many landlords won't accept credit cards and that many will also charge you the card's processing fees if you do choose to pay by card.

10. Phone a Friend

It's good to get additional opinions. Why? Because there are few processes more prone to emotional attachment than finding a home.

Imagine the following scenario. You've been looking for a new place for months and you've finally found that apartment that's in the right location. The landlord says he loves your dog as much as you do. The price is lower than you'd even dreamed it could be. Sure, you've never met the landlord, and he seems to always be traveling, but that's fine, right? Surely, you'll be able to get inside the place before you move in—he said he'll be back next week. And you've already paid a $250 "holding fee" via Venmo, so you're kind of already committed.

Tell your friends about the situation and let them tell you if things seem weird to them. Walk your friend through this list of risk factors and get a second opinion. When you're the one struggling to find the place and excited about the new opportunity, it's easy to let something slide. And when you've let one thing slide, it's easy to let another one, and then another one.

We're all guilty of getting emotionally invested in a decision sometimes, and this kind of decision is particularly risky in that way.

Be safe, phone a friend, and get an additional perspective.

Most people believe they're the kind of person who would never fall for a scam, especially when it involves something as important as a rental apartment. Scammers can be subtle and clever, though—more so than you might think. It's important to tread carefully and be cautious during every step of the process. Be sensitive to signs that things aren't quite right.

Remember: When it comes to fraud, it's better to be safe than sorry. If you are uncomfortable with a potential landlord for any reason, don't hesitate to move on to another rental.

1.6

WHAT KINDS OF PLACES ARE THERE?

Do you want a one-bedroom apartment? How about a studio? Ever considered a condo? What the #$%& is a condo, and how is it different from an apartment?

You've got options, and you've got lots of them. And the language used to talk about them can be confusing. Let's talk about the different types of rentals so you can understand the lingo when you're searching listings.

In this section, we'll give you a quick overview of a few of the most common kinds of rentals. That way, you'll be able to decide what type of apartment suits your specific needs best.

STUDIO/BACHELOR APARTMENT

A studio is an apartment in which the living room, the kitchen, and your sleeping space are all in a single room. This means that there are no interior walls within the apartment except those around the bathroom. (Bathroom walls are required by US housing law, so you should always have those.)

In other words: you might be able to reach out and touch your couch while you're cooking dinner. Cozy!

Pros	Cons
• Usually cheaper than apartments with dedicated bedrooms • Cheaper rent can allow you to live closer to things that are important to you • Easier to furnish, clean, and maintain a smaller space • Cheaper utilities, more energy efficient	• Harder to create a dedicated workspace in a studio if you work remotely • Private life is "on display" when you host because your bedroom is out in the open (your guests might see your dirty socks) • Smaller amounts of storage space • More difficult to live with a roommate or pets • Likely won't come with much, if any, closet space (so your guests might actually see **all** of your socks)

ONE-BEDROOM (OR A TWO- OR THREE-BEDROOM) APARTMENT

Unlike a studio apartment, apartments identified by their number of bedrooms come with one or more bedrooms sectioned off with walls and a closing door. These apartments often have the living area and the kitchen in the same room. The extra bedroom(s) means that they're somewhat bigger than a normal studio apartment.

Pros	Cons
• More space than a studio • Bedroom separates sleeping from waking life • More privacy for two or more people living together • Good for entertaining because of the dedicated living area • More storage space	• More expensive than a studio—the more bedrooms, the more expensive • Harder and more expensive to heat and cool than a studio due to increased square footage • More space to clean • Might need to live further from the city center to be able to afford the extra room

If you get stuck on deciding between a one-bedroom and a studio, there are a few key factors you should consider to make your decision:

- **Are you living with someone?** In a studio, two can be a crowd, even if your roommate is also your long-term partner. There's not a lot of privacy in an apartment with one main room, which means that things like telehealth appointments and other sensitive calls can be difficult.
- **What's your budget?** Studios are generally cheaper than one-bedrooms. This is mostly because they're smaller, but they're also more energy efficient, so your energy bills will be smaller in a studio than they would in a one-bedroom. If you're working with a smaller budget, a studio might be a better option.
- **Are you working from home?** If you're a remote worker, a one-bedroom will allow you to separate your workspace from either your sleeping or living space, and that could be beneficial for your mental health. There are a few ways around this in a studio, of course: you can erect dividers or find other ways to separate different spaces in your apartment. You'll just want to figure the cost of such equipment into your budget.
- **How often do you entertain other people?** If you entertain often, a one-bedroom is probably a better idea. In a studio, your

guests are more likely to see your private things because you'll sleep right in the open near (or on) your couch. If you don't entertain, though, maybe a studio is for you: it'll require less furniture and less cleaning.

SINGLE-FAMILY HOME

Single-family homes are what you're probably picturing when you think about American suburbia. A single-family home is a standalone house on its own plot of land, often with a front yard and backyard. It's designed to suit one family, with one kitchen and without sharing utilities with any other dwelling.

Some row houses and townhouses are considered single-family homes as long as they are separated from ground to roof by a wall. Such residences are referred to as "attached" single-family homes, whereas "unattached" or "detached" homes share no walls with any other residences.

TOWNHOME/TOWNHOUSE

A townhome or townhouse is a type of multistory dwelling that shares walls with other townhomes. They are normally taller and narrower than conventional single-family houses. You'll likely have some outdoor space when you rent a townhome: a backyard, front yard, a patio, or something similar. Like condos, townhomes are normally governed by a homeowner association (HOA). We'll talk about HOAs after we explain what a condo is.

CONDO

A condominium (or a condo) is defined by who owns it rather than the number of rooms it has. A condo is a building where each individual unit is separately owned, instead of all of the units in the building being owned by one landlord. The common areas of these buildings are owned and maintained by all of the owners together through their HOA. The units in a condo can be studios, one-bedrooms, or any other kind of apartment.

Because every individual unit in a condo is owned by a different person, the units will likely all look different. This isn't always true in an apartment building, where all of the units are owned by the same person or company—those units are often identical. The units in a condo, however, will represent the individual tastes of their owners. Depending on whether you like the owner's taste, this can be a good or bad thing.

When you rent a condo, you'll probably be renting from the individual owner of the condo, and that person will be your landlord. If this landlord owns many properties or doesn't live in the area, perhaps they've hired a property manager who will take care of things for them, and the property manager will be your contact for any day-to-day communications (like maintenance requests, for example).

Pros	Cons
• More personal feel to the apartment • HOA amenities and common areas • Usually updated more frequently than a normal apartment	• HOA fees and rules can be strict and difficult to abide by • Owner often doesn't live on-site, so repairs may take longer • You will have to deal with the "quirks" of the owner, like unique decor choices • Layout won't be consistent from condo to condo—you'll be in for something different depending on which unit you rent

WHAT IS A HOMEOWNER ASSOCIATION?

An HOA is an organization of people who own the homes in your community. They're common for people who live in townhomes, condos, or planned communities. The HOA's community of owners elects the people who lead the HOA.

An HOA's general job is to make sure that things are running smoothly in the community, but its exact range of responsibilities and the power it has will vary from place to place. Normally, an HOA creates and enforces the community's rules and regulations. These rules are called CC&Rs—or covenants, conditions, and restrictions. These will vary from HOA to HOA.

HOAs are also bound by their own set of rules, called bylaws. These bylaws regulate how the HOA runs meetings, holds elections, and does other things.

How Do HOAs Affect Me as a Renter?

As a renter, you won't be part of the HOA, but you'll still be bound by its rules. (These will probably be written into your lease, as per the requirements of the HOA.) If you rent directly from the owner of your property, then your landlord is likely part of the HOA.

You'll also be paying the HOA's fees in one way or another: either the fees will be factored into your rent, or there will be a clause in your lease stating that you have to pay them separately.

If you break a rule, the HOA cannot take direct action against you because you are a tenant and not an HOA member. Instead, it will notify your landlord. Then, it's your landlord's job to handle the situation. They might have written into your lease that you have to pay them back for fees incurred related to noncompliance with the HOA's rules.

What Kinds of HOA Rules Will I Be Expected to Follow?

Rules will vary depending on the HOA and the community in question, but here are some of the classics:

- No alterations/additions are permitted on the outside of the unit or building
- No loud parties
- No pets (or heavy restrictions on what pets are allowed)
- Restrictions on what kind of vehicle you can have and how many vehicles you can have
- Restrictions on how, where, and when trash is discarded

If you're thinking about living in a community with an HOA, you'll want to do some research on what the HOA's rules are and think about whether they're in line with your lifestyle. There might be an HOA out there that is perfect for you.

You should also understand the HOA's rules around renting. Sadly, there are some HOAs that do not allow renting, and your landlord may or may not know if theirs is one of them. You should understand if the HOA governing your new home even allows rentals. This is one reason why it's essential to make sure you thoroughly understand your lease before you sign—you might find out later that the HOA rules say you can't rent your place! Make sure you read everything over, talk to your landlord, and even reach out to the HOA to prevent this from happening.

Remember: Understanding the pros and cons of each apartment style will save you time, energy, and probably even money. Decide what you'd like ahead of time.

1.7

BUDGETING AND KNOWING WHAT YOU CAN AFFORD

You'll want to figure out your budget before you start looking for a rental so that you have a realistic idea of what you can afford.

It should be straightforward determining how much of your monthly budget you can put toward rent, but that's not always the case due to two big unknowns:

- What do you qualify for? Many landlords will require your monthly income to be three or four times the rent or your annual income to be forty times your monthly rent, but this can vary widely. What will your landlord require?
- What are the costs you're required to pay on top of the rent, such as utilities, parking fees, pet rent, and others? These can be substantial and add up to 25 percent or more over and above the rent.

There's some old advice that you should be willing to spend up to 30 percent of your income on rent, but that's very personal and depends a lot on where you live.

There are some relatively rich renters living in New York or San Francisco who are paying 50 percent or more of their income on rent, and that's fine for them. In other markets, like Detroit or Cleveland, you might find you can get so much rental for your money that 15 or 20 percent of your income is more than enough to get you a great place.

Let's help you figure out your budget by going through the various expenses associated with your rental apartment or house and work up to what makes sense for you.

UP-FRONT FEES

To start, there are a bunch of up-front fees that you should be aware of and ready to pay—and then the ongoing rent and other expenses that you'll need to pay every month. Let's break them down.

The Application

Cost: $35–$100
Timing: When you decide you're serious about a place

The first thing you'll have to pay is an application fee. Why do they charge this? Landlords, too, face up-front costs, such as paying someone to do the application screening, but the fee is not just for recovering their costs. Forcing you to put a little money down helps them identify who's really serious about the place.

In the grand scheme of the new rental process, this is far from your biggest expense, but it can add up if you have to submit several applications, so it's important to apply only for rentals you're serious about.

Most importantly, remember that most application processes include a "hard pull" on your credit,* which can lower your credit score—another reason to keep applications to a minimum.

The Holding Fee/Deposit

Cost: As low as $100 and as high as one week's rent
Timing: Usually after you've been approved but before you've signed the lease

A landlord may charge a holding fee to take the property off the market even before you sign the lease. It typically holds the rental for a couple of days until you can get the lease signed and come up with the other funds required. It might hold the place for as little as twenty-four hours or as long as a week, but it does buy you a little time to read the lease and get ready to put the full deposit down.

Usually, this fee is nonrefundable if you back out of the place. If you move in, it's typically used to reduce other move-in costs, such as payment of first month's rent or the security deposit.

First and/or Last Month's Rent

Cost: One or two month's rent
Timing: When you sign the lease

This is prepayment of rent. It's quite typical to have to pay the first month's rent, and in some places, they'll also ask you to pay the last month's rent up front.

It's unusual, but not unheard of, to have to pay first and last month's rent in addition to a security deposit. More typically, landlords will require one or the other.

* A "hard pull" is when a lender, like a landlord, checks your credit report. Usually, this has a negative impact on your credit score because it indicates that you're applying to borrow money. A "soft pull" is when you check your own credit report or score, which doesn't impact your credit score in any way.

Security Deposit

Cost: Usually (but not always) one month's rent
Timing: When you sign the lease *or* by the time you get the keys

A security deposit is a payment that is held by your landlord as security in case you damage your rental. Depending on the condition of your rental when you move out, you may get some or all of the security deposit back. (See Section 5.4 for more information about how to get your security deposit back.)

Move-In/Move-Out/Administration Fees

Cost: $150–$400
Timing: When you move in or out; could be added to the up-front payment with the first month's rent or added to a later rent invoice

These fees are intended to cover the use of facilities (booking an elevator or loading dock, etc.). They are generally nonrefundable, but in some cases, there is a security-deposit component of the fee that will be refunded when you hand back elevator keys or other items that you may have used in your move.

Pet Deposit

Cost: $300–$800 or a percentage of a month's rent (often 30–80 percent)
Timing: Before you move your pet into the rental

A pet deposit is something like an extra security deposit. We all love our pets, and surely they would never damage your apartment, right?

Unfortunately, that's not the way landlords see it. The good news about renting now is that many places will allow you to have a pet. Ten years ago, that was not the case. The bad news is that there is an extra cost to the landlord as a result of you having a pet, and they're looking to recover those costs or protect themselves from risk with fees like this. To learn more about the extra cost and why landlords generally don't like to have pets in their apartments, turn to Section 3.1.

Broker Fees

Cost: 8–12 percent of a year's rent
Timing: Prior to moving in

In some markets, most notably New York City, there's another huge expense—the cost for the broker who helped you find the place. This is a big, nonrefundable fee.

These folks work hard for their money and can be a big help in the rental search. But the cost for their service is very substantial, so if you'd like to avoid it, look for "no-fee rentals" or something similar and always be sure to ask up front if there's a broker fee.

OTHER COMMON ONGOING EXPENSES

We all know about the rent, but there's a range of other expenses you will have to pay over the course of your rental. Make sure to know what you're on the hook for so you understand your total cost to live in that rental.

1. Utilities

Depending on your rental and where you live, utilities can be a minor expense or a big one. For example, average water bills in 2022 in West Virginia were $105/month, but in North Carolina they averaged $20.[3]

The typical utilities in your home or apartment that you need to be prepared for are electricity, water, gas, sewer, trash, internet access, and cable.

In some rentals (particularly large apartment complexes), there are utility-like fees that may be due to the landlord. They include trash pickup, pest control, and amenity fees.

Your future landlord should be able to help you get ballpark estimates on all utilities, whether they're paid to the landlord or not. In some places, like Chicago, there is a formal disclosure for some or all utility rates, but in virtually all places, the landlord can give you a sense of what other residents pay.

Be prepared to take that information with a grain of salt, though, because the landlord may not know the exact numbers that the last resident paid and because your use of the place could be very different from that of prior users.

As a general rule of thumb, folks moving into an apartment should budget $150 to $200 per month for utilities, but a lot depends on the place, where in the country you live, and the options you choose (blazing-fast internet, anyone?).

2. Parking

Just like free lunch, there's rarely such a thing as free parking. Most apartments, particularly in urban locations, will charge for every parking spot.

With many suburban apartment complexes, you can get one spot for free but will need to pay for any additional ones you may need.

Prices vary wildly for parking. We've seen them as low as $75 and as high as $600 per month. Make sure you know what you need and ask up front so you know what you're signing up for.

Usually, with single-family home rentals, there is no parking charge.

3. Pet Rent

Some places have pet deposits (a larger, up-front, refundable payment), and some have pet rent. Pet rent is a monthly charge for all pet owners, usually assessed on a per-pet basis.

In terms of cost, pet rent for cats is typically $25–$50/month, and for dogs, it's often $30–$80/month.

4. Renters Insurance

Some landlords will require you to have renters insurance, and they may try to sell you that insurance from a company they have a relationship with. Maybe that's the right one for you, but you can also look around and see other options.

Renters insurance can be as little as $5/month or as much as $20/month, depending on what you sign up for. Check out Section 4.2 for all the details on renters insurance.

WHAT DOES IT ALL ADD UP TO?

Let's look at the costs for DeAnne, a renter we spoke to who recently moved into an apartment in Atlanta.

Here's what she was on the hook for as a result of her apartment search.

DeAnne's Up-Front Costs

Expense Item	Date Paid	One-Time Cost
Application 1 (Rental 1)	July 20	$48
Application 2 (Rental 2)	July 24	$45
Holding Deposit (Refunded)	July 24	$250
First Month's Rent	July 27	$1,275
Security Deposit	July 27	$1,275
Elevator (Move-In Fee)	July 27	$100
Pet Deposit	July 27	$500
Total Up-Front Costs		$3,243

DeAnne had to come up with a total of $3,243 in order to rent an apartment with a rent of $1,275/month. Surprised? Most of us are when the time comes, but that won't be you, renting whiz, because you're reading this book.

Remember to gather the numbers so you can do your own version of the chart above to calculate how much you'll have to pay before you move into a place.

Also note the dates in the chart above. DeAnne didn't have much time to come up with the funds to rent the place—just three days from the time she was approved.

When it comes to ongoing monthly costs, you should tally those up, too. Here's what they looked like for DeAnne.

DeAnne's Ongoing Monthly Costs

Expense Item	Monthly Cost
Rent	$1,275
Water & Sewer	$40
Electricity	$75
Gas	$60
Trash	(Paid by landlord)
Pet Rent	$40
Parking	$90
Renters Insurance	$12
Internet	$99
Total	$1,691

Again, DeAnne's example illustrates how many additional costs there are in addition to the base rent—more than $400 extra each month, in her case. Doing this exercise for yourself can help you make sure you're ready for the full costs of the place that you're renting.

HOW TO FIGURE OUT THE RIGHT BUDGET FOR YOU

We wish we could tell you that there's some magic or foolproof rule of thumb for determining your best budget.

Unfortunately, there are no real shortcuts to figuring this out for you. The best way is to take a look at your monthly income and do the math for yourself.

How do you do the math? Start with your income. If you're paying rent right now, is it uncomfortable for you, from a financial perspective? Or is it comfortable, and you feel like you could spend a little more? That "feeling" is an important one; it tells you if you have room in your budget or if you need to find a way to reduce costs in your new place.

If you're not currently in a rental—maybe you're living with your parents—then try living for a month or two without the money you would earmark for rent. Maybe start with 30 percent of your income or another number that makes sense to you given where you are and what market rates look like. This serves two purposes. First, it tells you how comfortable your imagined rent number would be, and second, it helps you save the money necessary to take possession of your place.

Once you have a sense of what your budget can handle, make sure you do all the math when it comes to evaluating your potential new home, as DeAnne did. Add up all the costs and compare them to your projected budget. When the two match, then you've found your answer.

Remember: You know best what you can afford—there's no rule that can take into consideration your unique situation.

1.8

ARE THERE GOOD AND BAD TIMES OF THE YEAR TO SEARCH?

There are better and worse times of the year to search for and move into a new place.

The best time of year to plan a move is in the winter, around December or January. The worst time of year is in the summer or the early fall.

Why is this? Rental rates are seasonal, so they move up and down depending on the time of year. It's not a small fluctuation in rent, either—the difference in cost can be 10 percent or more. That's the difference between a $900 apartment and a $1,000 apartment. That's nothing to sneeze at, especially when you start adding up what you would save on rent over the whole year (a $100 difference in rent means an extra $1,200 per year—wow!). This fluctuation occurs because fewer people want to move during the winter: school is still in session, and the weather can get nasty.

You might be thinking, "But rent is always going up!"—and you'd be right. Rent usually goes up from year to year, but month to month, it behaves differently. Take a look at the following chart to see what we mean. You can see that the rent drops in January and February, although it generally goes up from year to year. The overall rising cost of rent makes it even more important to take advantage of dips in price like the ones in the winter because you'll save money over time, and the rising cost won't hit you quite as hard.

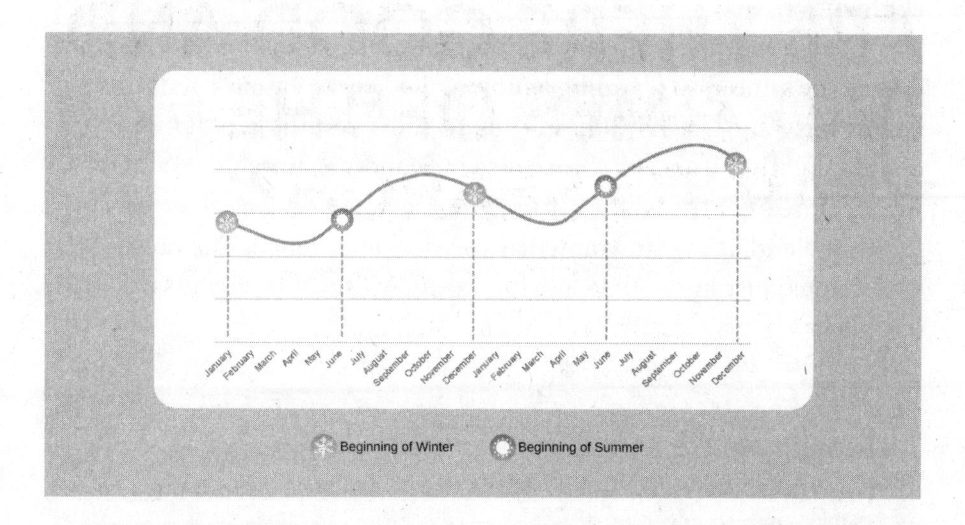

If you start to rent a place in January and you've signed a twelve-month lease, you'll be due for a lease renewal the following January. That means you'll benefit from lower rent yet again. So if you can stick to a pattern of renting in the winter, you'll benefit in the long and the short term from the lower cost of rent during that time of year.

But what if your lease ends during the summer? Don't worry, you still have a few options. You can ask your landlord to extend your lease until January. They might not, but you'll never know if you don't try. Alternatively, you can try to sign a shorter lease that ends in December or January. Your landlord will usually want to avoid that, so you'll open up a way to negotiate. You might not even have to plan a move right away.

Once your lease ends in the winter, you can move somewhere else to take advantage of the lower rent or negotiate with your landlord for lower rent in your current place.

There are a few downsides to moving in the winter, of course. Breaking your lease early can be difficult and expensive, and usually you don't want to do that (see Section 5.5 for more information). You might have to move in the snow, depending on where you live. And there are generally fewer rentals available in the winter months, particularly in snowy places. (There will be fewer people looking, though, so you might face less competition.)

A few other pros: Movers are normally less expensive and less busy during the winter, so planning a move will likely be easier. Landlords will be less busy, too, so they'll have time to show you the rental more thoroughly, and they'll also be able to do a little more maintenance and repair work before or at the start of your lease.

In the end, it's up to you when you decide to move. The power is in your hands. Just know that moving in the wintertime might save you a few bucks.

Remember: Yes, rent is always rising, but those yearly dips can help you save big if you're able to take advantage of them.

1.9

FAIR HOUSING LAW

No one wants to experience discrimination during their search for a rental. We certainly hope it's not a problem you face at any point during your search.

But, because housing discrimination still happens, we want to make sure that if you do experience it, you know what to do next. In this section, we're going to talk about the Fair Housing Act, go over some common forms of housing discrimination, and discuss what you can do if someone discriminates against you during your rental search.

It's important to remember that we are not lawyers, and if, after reading this, you think you've been subjected to fair-housing discrimination, you should contact your local fair-housing council or the Department of Housing and Urban Development (HUD) at www.hud.gov for expert help.

WHAT IS THE FAIR HOUSING ACT?

The Fair Housing Act, or the FHA, is the big star of this section. It's a federal law that protects people from discrimination when they're participating in lots of different housing-related activities. These could include looking for a rental, living in your rental, buying a home, or getting a mortgage.

What Classes Are Protected?

First, let's talk about what a protected class is. Protected classes are groups of people who share a particular attribute that causes them to get special protection under the law while renting.

These categories of protected classes are covered by the FHA:

- Race
- Color
- National origin
- Religion
- Sex (including gender identity and sexual orientation)
- Familial status (the presence of minor children)
- Disability

Depending on your state or municipality, there may be additional classes protected. To the best of our knowledge, Madison, Wisconsin, takes the cake with thirty-seven protected classes, so keep in mind that the number of protected classes can be quite extensive, depending on where you live.[4] Some of the most common additional protected classes are source of income, marital status, and military status.

What Types of Housing Are Covered Under the Act?

Most housing is covered by the FHA, but there are some significant exceptions. HUD's website lists the following examples of the limited circumstances when housing may not be covered under the FHA:[5]

- Owner-occupied buildings with no more than four units
- Single-family houses sold or rented by an owner without the use of an agent, if the owner doesn't own more than three single-family houses
- Housing operated by religious organizations for the organization's members, such as a monastery or convent

- Private clubs that offer housing limited to occupancy by members

Not all housing in these examples is exempt, but depending on the circumstances, it might be.

WHAT DOES DISCRIMINATION LOOK LIKE?

If you look at HUD's website, you'll be able to find a full list of the various discriminatory actions that are illegal under the FHA.

These include things like refusing to rent or sell housing, evicting a tenant or their guest, or assigning someone a particular building or section of a building, all when based on that person's membership in a legally protected class. The list is expansive, however, so if you're concerned about being discriminated against, it is best to read it yourself directly from the source (www.hud.gov).

Here are a few examples of the more common types of housing discrimination today:

- A property-management company that writes "no children" on its advertisements because it does not want to rent to families with children.
- A landlord who assigns all tenants of the same race to a particular hallway or section of their building.
- A leasing agent who tells someone with a mobility disability that they can't rent anything above the first floor.
- A landlord who treats a Muslim resident differently from a Christian resident when both have not paid their rent.

Of course, these are only a few different examples of housing discrimination. Discrimination comes in many different forms, dependent both on context and on the previous patterns of behavior of the people involved.

HOW DO YOU KNOW IF SOMEONE IS DISCRIMINATING AGAINST YOU?

It might be difficult to tell if you're experiencing discrimination because it isn't always obvious. Here are a few of our best tips:

- **Take notes.** During and after your conversations with landlords, leasing agents, building managers, and anyone else involved in your rental process, take notes. Write down dates, times, content, and any important quotes from your interaction. Also, make note of the names and job titles of anyone you are in contact with. If any decisions are made, make sure you get them in writing. This is good practice for tracking your rental search regardless, but it also can provide evidence that will help your case if you find yourself needing to file a complaint.
- **Consider the language of the interaction.** Sometimes, the way that people speak to you can tip you off about potential discrimination. Maybe your landlord asked if you were pregnant or what your nationality is. These questions might seem innocent, but it's possible that they're looking to avoid renting to you. Discriminatory language takes more forms than just asking about your identity, however. Perhaps a landlord mentioned that there weren't a lot of "people like you" in the building. They might have also suggested that they weren't sure you'd be "comfortable" in the area or that the "community" might not be a "good fit" for you. All of these statements, and statements like them, can carry discriminatory subtext. Again, make sure you write everything down.
- **Watch for new obstacles in the process.** Unexpected problems are often indicators that you're experiencing discrimination. For instance, you might be completely qualified to rent a unit, apply for it, get denied, and then find out it's still available online. You might even be told that an apartment is not available, when it clearly is, before you even get the chance to apply for it. Or maybe a landlord intends to rent to you until they meet you in

person and learn your race, at which point they reject you. All of these obstacles could be examples of perfectly legitimate rental-business procedures, but they could also point toward unlawful housing discrimination.

WHAT DO YOU DO IF YOU EXPERIENCE HOUSING DISCRIMINATION?

You can reach out for help from the federal government if you experience housing discrimination. For instance, HUD has a lot of useful information about what to do if you think you've experienced unlawful discrimination in a housing transaction. Most states and many local jurisdictions (at the county or city level) also have fair-housing or civil-rights offices. The helpfulness of these state or local government organizations will vary depending on where you live, but you should be able to find them with a little research online.

Many areas also have private fair-housing advocacy groups (often called "fair-housing councils") that will be interested in investigating your concerns. That investigation might involve sending out "testers" posing as housing seekers to the person or company who discriminated against you in order to find evidence of discrimination. Dwellsy has a listing of many of the tenant advocacy groups around the country on our blog at Dwellsy.com/blog/renterorganizations.

You can also file a complaint with HUD online, through the mail, or over the phone. It will investigate your complaint and decide whether what you have experienced violates the law. Retaliation against you because you filed a fair-housing complaint is also illegal.

If you decide to file a complaint with HUD, you will be asked to provide the following, per its website:

- A timeline of events, starting with the first contact you had with the person or entity you believe violated your rights

- The locations of events
- Any people who were present when events occurred
- Any other people who might have information related to your complaint
- Any relevant documents

HUD will then assign an investigator to gather information from the location where you experienced discrimination. HUD acts as a neutral party during the investigation, although it will attempt "conciliation" (settlement by a resolution that suits everyone involved). You're not required to agree to a settlement.

In some cases, HUD may decide to bring a civil-rights case before an administrative-law judge or a federal-court trial judge based on the findings of the investigation. If that happens, HUD ceases to be a neutral party and brings the case on your behalf, without any fees or costs to you. The complaint will be handled by lawyers from HUD's own Office of General Counsel or the US Department of Justice and decided by a judge or jury, depending on the forum.

Of course, we hope that you never have to experience any of these things during your rental process. If anything does happen, though, we want you to feel prepared and not be afraid to report any unlawful behavior you believe you've encountered so that no one else is discriminated against.

Remember: Discrimination is never okay. If you're discriminated against during your housing search process, please advocate for yourself, and don't be afraid to ask for help.

Section 2

LET'S FIND THAT PLACE

Here's where the rubber meets the road. You've read Section 1. You understand how your landlord thinks. You're ready to dodge and weave around the scammers. You know the kinds of places available to rent, how to budget, and the best times of year to find yourself a place. You're on your way to becoming a real renting expert!

Now, let's get going with the search, which is likely what you're here for. In this section, we'll walk you through how to conduct a search from start to finish.

We're going to start with some of the foundational work that you want to do to get ready for the search.

Why on earth should you do things even before you start searching?

In order to get the place you're dreaming of, speed is of the essence. You need to be ready to move and move fast when the right place presents itself.

And if you aren't ready, you're going to lose it to someone who *is* ready. Don't lose to that person; *be* that person.

2.1

NAIL DOWN THE BASICS OF YOUR SEARCH

As in all things, you need to pick a place to start. And with finding your next place, getting started can seem daunting. But it doesn't have to be.

Like you'll hear us say over and over again in this book, just take things one step at a time. In this section, we'll talk about where you could live, what kind of apartment you want, what your budget is, and how many roommates you want to have (if any).

The overall goal of this section is to help you come up with a list of priorities to take to any rental search engine (but especially Dwellsy!) Remember: no one can decide what your priorities are or what you're willing to be flexible about except for you. Once you've got the basics down, you won't waste any time or money on apartments or houses that don't make sense for you.

Let's ease into this with some easy-ish questions so you can start to figure out what you're looking for.

Q1: WHERE DO YOU WANT TO LIVE?

This sounds like a simple question, right? And it should be, but where you live determines so many other things that it's worth delving into this for a minute.

Ever hear the old saying about real estate—that it's about three things: location, location, location? That's not completely true, but it is mostly true.

Location determines the cost of your place, the type of rental available to you, the length of your commute to your work, your distance from friends and family, the nature and type of entertainment options around you, and your proximity to all manner of things that might matter to you.

Love movies? Maybe the most important thing for you is to be close to a great movie theater. Have a best friend in town? Maybe you want to live super close to them. Taking care of someone? Maybe you need to be near them. Working 24/7? Maybe you want to live close to work so you can easily stumble home from work at midnight to catch some sleep.

Maybe you already know where you want to be because you want to stay in the same city or neighborhood, or you know exactly where you're going to move. If that's the case, feel free to move on to the next section.

But for most of us, thinking hard about location is an important place to start because it dictates so many other things and helps us understand other constraints.

Keep in mind, though, that there is no perfect location—only trade-offs.

If, for example, you want to be in Midtown Manhattan, then that means you're going to be spending a bundle on a small place with no outdoor space and maybe living with a couple of roommates. This could be the perfect living experience for you. Unless you need a backyard for your Bernese mountain dog (Jonas's dream dog!)—in that case, you need to think a little differently about location.

Or, if you want to be close to your parents' place in the burbs, then you likely have lots of options in terms of space, but you may struggle to find great choices because it can be more challenging to find single-family home rentals (don't worry, we've devoted a whole section to that—Section 3.4).

Q2: DO YOU HAVE A PET?

Man, we love our pets. Furry, scaly, or otherwise, they make great company and can truly turn a house or an apartment into a home. But not all landlords love them. We have a whole section on how to navigate pet ownership and care in rentals (Section 3.1), but for now, it's important to note that if you have a pet, it can be a very big deal to a landlord and can dictate which places are available to you and which are not.

In general, cats are easiest, small dogs are next, and big dogs and exotic pets (snakes, rodents, llamas, etc.) are much more challenging to house in rentals.

Why is this question number two, you ask? Because while most renters have a level of flexibility in their living choices, pets are one area where there is relatively little. If you have a dog, your likelihood of giving up Fido for even the greatest apartment is pretty low. So, you need to put this consideration up front as you think about your search and understand how it will influence where you might call home in the end.

Again, this pet business is important, so we're here for you. Check Section 3.1 for all the details.

Q3: WHAT'S YOUR BUDGET, AND HOW MUCH FINANCIAL FLEXIBILITY DO YOU HAVE?

For most people, the cost of living is nonnegotiable. You want to be able to afford both rent and groceries, after all.

Using sites like Dwellsy's Rent Maps (Dwellsy.com/rentmaps) can help you get some solid numbers on the cost of rent in any particular city, and other resources, like NerdWallet and BestPlaces.net, have cost-of-living calculators that will give you a sense of the rest of the costs involved in living in a certain place.

With these tools, you can decide where you're able to afford the rent, put food on the table, supply kibble for Fido, pay your student-loan bills, and maybe even have a little bit of fun, too.

If you haven't already read Section 1.7, we go into detail there about what your budget might need to be and what your rental might cost you.

Having a sense of what rent might be in a place is important, but you also need to know what you might be able to afford. And that, of course, brings us to . . .

Q4: WHAT ARE YOU PLANNING TO DO FOR WORK?

Your work dictates a few different things in the apartment search:

- It helps set your budget.
- It helps you think about location. For example, do you need to come and go from work frequently? Is the commute a real nightmare? Maybe it's really important to live close to work. Maybe you work from home and need a quiet place for focus.
- It helps you think about the type of landlord you want to look for. Landlords like to get the rent consistently, so if you don't have a full-time job, or if you don't have a job lined up yet, you may need to be a little more creative in the rental search.

Don't have a job lined up? In that case, you're going to have to think about the job market in the city you're considering. Are there plenty of jobs there in your field? If not, you'll want to be sure you have a backup plan in place. Maybe you're in a position to switch fields, or maybe you know someone who is capable of getting you a job. These are all things you'll want to think about well ahead of time because most landlords will want to know that you have a steady source of income.

Q5: HOW MUCH DOES WEATHER MATTER TO YOU?

The weather can have a definite impact on your mood. Maybe you'd love a little more sunshine, or maybe you're craving snow. It's something to consider when you decide where you might want to live.

If you're thinking about moving to a city with a very different climate, it's a good idea to consider the cost of clothes and gear if you don't already have them. For example, if you're living in Hawaii and considering a move to New York, you'll want to think about a winter wardrobe—the prices for just a winter coat can be hefty.

Looking up the climate in the area you're considering is always a good move. A friend from the area who's willing to talk to you about the weather throughout the year can be even more helpful.

Q6: HOW IMPORTANT ARE CULTURE AND ACTIVITIES TO YOU?

What is there to do around the city you're considering? If you have certain hobbies where you live now, you might want to think about cities where you can keep them going once you move. Maybe you love to swim in the ocean, so you want a city near the beach. Maybe a hopping nightlife is for you, and your ideal city has a downtown with lots of restaurants and bars.

Q7: HOW CLOSE DO YOU WANT TO BE TO FRIENDS AND FAMILY?

Lots of folks have parents to take care of or friends they don't want to live apart from. Or maybe you're looking to get a little distance between where you grew up and your next stage of life. Either way, it makes sense to consider whether it's important to you that you're physically near those you love.

Maybe there's only a certain distance away from your hometown that you feel comfortable with, and you need to work within those parameters. On the other hand, maybe you're excited to move somewhere where you don't know a single person! It's all up to you. But either way, it's something to think about ahead of time.

Q8: WHAT ELSE MATTERS TO YOU?

The list of things that could potentially matter to you is endless and unique to you. Maybe you've hand-washed your last dish and will never go without a dishwasher again. Maybe you need a garage so you can work on restoring your '64 Mustang.

What matters is that you do a little thinking and try to figure out what your priorities are so you can take them into consideration from the very beginning of your rental search.

Remember: Overwhelmed by all of the different factors at play? Take this section question by question and, eventually, a cohesive picture of what you need will emerge.

2.2

FIGURE OUT YOUR PRIORITIES

Having answered some of the basic questions in the previous section, how do you think about how an apartment might actually match with your needs?

It can be overwhelming to keep track of all of the different rentals and balance out their pros and cons. You might find yourself hopelessly buried in information. Which rental was the closest to a grocery store, again? And which one was in that neighborhood you liked a lot? There can be so much to keep tabs on.

That's why the team at Dwellsy has created its decision matrix to help you easily visualize and weigh all of that dense info.

A decision matrix is a decision-making tool in the form of a chart, with rows and columns. You fill it out with information about the rentals you're interested in and list the criteria that matter the most to you. The decision matrix will help you weigh out the pros and cons, and it will also provide a handy visual so you can easily see all of the data right in front of you. By using the matrix, you'll be able to tell which rental is best for you in an objective sense.

Okay, we know this all sounds kind of nerdy. If you're not a graphs-and-numbers person, it might be hard to visualize. Don't worry: we won't leave you in the dust.

First, you're going to want to download Dwellsy's decision matrix. You can find it at Dwellsy.com/blog/renter-tip-use-a-decision-matrix/. This ready-made template is set up to do most of the work for you.

Next, we're going to walk you through exactly how to fill it out, and we'll also explain what each part of the spreadsheet means. You'll be an expert decision-matrix filler-outer by the time we're done!

FACTORS YOU MIGHT INCLUDE IN YOUR DECISION MATRIX

Every renter prioritizes different things when they're looking for a rental. You might really care about having a dishwasher, but another person might care more about having a washer and dryer. A place with pet rent might be a total no-go for you but not a dealbreaker for someone else. These kinds of criteria are the things you can put into a decision matrix in order to get some help weighing out your options.

These are a few of the things you're probably thinking about:

Size (e.g., square footage)	Security deposit cost	Central air (AC and heat)	Commute to work
Layout (e.g., single story, two story)	Pet policy	Natural light (e.g., windows)	Outdoor area (e.g., patio, balcony
Subletting options	Dishwasher	Lighting (built in)	Community amenities (e.g., doorman, gym)

Remember, only you know what's most important to you. It's worth taking a moment to look this list over and decide what you're going to prioritize.

FILLING OUT A DECISION MATRIX

So, what does a decision matrix actually look like when it's all fleshed out? Here's a sample using fictional apartments:

Rental Decision Matrix

An efficient way to choose your next home.

RENTAL ADDRESS		500 Hudson Yards		The Wheningold		123 Park Ave ★	
DECISION FACTORS	Weight of Factor	Unweighted Score	Weighted Score	Unweighted Score	Weighted Score	Unweighted Score	Weighted Score
Dishwasher	4	5	20	3	15	5	20
Monthly Rent	4	3	12	4	12	1	4
Size (e.g. square footage)	3	3	9	2	6	3	9
Layout (e.g. single story)	2	2	4	4	8	3	6
Pet Policy	1	0	0	0	0	0	0
Lease Duration	2	4	8	3	12	3	6
Renewal Terms	2	3	6	2	6	3	6
Security Deposit	3	3	9	2	6	2	6
Natural Light	3	5	15	3	15	5	15
Lighting (built-in)	2	1	2	2	2	5	10
Water Pressure	3	4	12	1	4	5	15
Neighborhood	4	5	20	2	10	2	8
Commute to Work	4	1	4	1	1	5	20
Outdoor Area (e.g. patio, balcony)	1	0	0	4	0	0	0
Central Air (AC and Heat)	3	4	12	3	12	5	15
Building Type (e.g. Townhouse, high-rise)	1	1	1	1	1	0	0
Community Amenities (e.g. gym, doorman)	1	4	4	0	0	5	5
Refigerator	5	5	25	3	15	5	25
In-Unit Washer/Drier	3	4	12	5	20	5	15
Elevator	2	2	4	5	10	4	8
TOTAL WEIGHTED SCORE		179		155		193 ★	

Let's break this chart down into its basic components so that you understand it completely.

In the topmost row of the chart, you can see the different addresses of all of your potential rentals.

In the leftmost column of the chart, you can see all of the different factors that you want to consider in making your final decision. You can list anything you want here, from location to amenities. A few examples from our chart include "Dishwasher," "Lease Duration," and "Neighborhood."

In the next column over, you'll assign each factor a certain weight, depending on how important it is to you, from 0 to 5 (0 being the lowest, 5 being the highest). For instance, say that a dishwasher is pretty important to you but not a top-shelf priority. You might assign "Dishwasher" a weight of 4. The type of building, on the other hand, doesn't matter much to you—you don't care a whole lot whether you live in a townhouse or a studio. You might assign "Building Type" a value of 1, then. You'll use this weight later when calculating your final score for each rental.

In the columns labeled "Unweighted Score" under each individual rental, you'll score the unit on each factor you have listed, also from 0 to 5 (0 being the lowest, 5 being the highest). Say the natural light in 500 Hudson Yards is excellent; you'd give "Natural Light" under "500 Hudson Yards" a 5, just as we've done in the example. The "Monthly Rent" for the same rental is middling, however, so we've given that a 3. For each rental and each factor, you'd fill out these "Unweighted Score" columns until they're all done.

Then, we can move on to determining your weighted scores for each rental. To do this, you'll take the weight of each factor and multiply that by its unweighted score. Let's take "Natural Light" in 500 Hudson Yards as an example. We gave it a weight of 3 and a score of 5, and 3 x 5 = 15. Therefore, we ended up with a final weighted score of 15 on "Natural Light" for 500 Hudson Yards. As another example, let's look at "Monthly Rent" for the same rental: we gave it a weight of 4 and a score of 3, so by multiplying them, we end up with 12. Do this for each factor and each rental until all of the "Weighted Score" columns are full. (We know—it's a lot of math! Downloading Dwellsy's Google Sheets version of the matrix or using a calculator will help. You can find and download the Google Sheets version here: Dwellsy.com/blog/renter-tip-use-a-decision-matrix/.)

By adding up the weighted scores for each rental (again, a calculator or Google Sheets version is best here), you'll get each unit's final score. From here, it's easy: the biggest number wins! 123 Park Avenue is the winner in our example.

THE MATRIX WILL DO THE HARD WORK FOR YOU

If you use Dwellsy's Google Sheets matrix, the formulas in the sheet will do the hard work. The weighted scores will magically appear in the white column, calculated using the weights you provided and your unweighted score. All of the rentals' total scores will appear down below. And bam, you've got your objective answer: highest score. Pretty cool, right? (We know. We're nerds.)

You can continue to change these numbers as you find and tour rentals and get a feel for them. It's good to start on this stuff early on in the rental process, which is why we're giving it to you now. You can start to fill your matrix out with the information on the listings you find.

Once you know which apartments you want to rent, you can start reaching out to landlords in order to set up tours.

TOO MUCH FOR YOU?

We know, we know. Nerd central over here. If using a spreadsheet to track this is too much for you, there's nothing here you can't replicate with a single sheet of paper and a pencil. You can chart this out yourself and add all the places you discover by using a pro/con list or whatever method suits your fancy. We also find it helpful to have photos of each property so you can remember which one is which. Either save them in your favorites list on Dwellsy or keep a separate file of photos from listings or that you took yourself, but if you do this, make sure to name or label photos so you can remember the address for each later on!

Remember: Find a way to stay organized that works for you, and remember that prioritizing what's important to you will make it more likely that you'll find a great home.

2.3

GET YOUR (PAPER) DUCKS IN A ROW

A BIG PART OF THE RENTAL SEARCH

If you're wondering exactly what kind of documents you need for a rental application, we've got you covered. Of course, every application will be a little bit different, based on what the landlord wants to know about you. But here are the most common things you'll need to bring when you tour the apartment in order to apply (and you should be ready to apply immediately after the tour):

- Pay stubs or bank statements for the previous two or three months
- Driver's license, state ID, passport, or residency card
- Social security number
- Checkbook
- If you have a car, vehicle registration and insurance
- If you have a pet, pet registration (if you have it)
- Proof of renters insurance (if you have it)

We suggest getting these documents together beforehand. That way, you're not scrambling to find something at the last minute.

CHECK YOUR CREDIT SCORE

We know that looking at your credit score is often no fun. The thing is, it's an important part of the application process. A landlord is going to want to know what the situation is if your credit score isn't too hot. They're also going to want to know that you're willing to face up to the situation and find a good solution.

You'll want to know what your credit score is before you even apply so that it doesn't take you by surprise. If your score will negatively affect your application, at least you'll have time to think about how to offset it.

Not sure how to check your credit score? Credit-score companies and the programs they offer change more often than you may think, so we maintain an overview of the options on the Dwellsy blog (dwellsy.com/blog/credit), where you can find sources for a free credit report and paid options. Most people use AnnualCreditReport.com, a site that allows you a free credit report once a year from each of the three major credit bureaus.

Having a bad credit score (or no credit score at all) is such a common problem that we have an entire section about credit in this book (see Section 3.3).

CLEAN UP YOUR SOCIAL MEDIA

If you were applying for a job, you'd probably take a good look at your social media to make sure it's spotless. You'll want to do the same when you're applying for an apartment. There's a pretty good chance that your landlord will Google your name and take at least a cursory glance at your socials. You don't want to have anything on there that might turn them off.

What kinds of things? Posts about drugs, alcohol, and/or parties could make a landlord less willing to have you as a tenant because they might not want to rent to someone who'll bring those things into their rental. The same goes for smoking. Scroll down your socials and Google yourself to see what comes up.

MAKE SURE YOUR REFERENCE LETTERS ARE EXCELLENT

It's likely that you've had to pick people to write reference letters for you before. If that's the case, then you know the drill. You'll want to pick people who think highly of you, normally those you're acquainted with in a professional capacity.

If you have a good relationship with any of your former landlords, they would be good people to ask. They know all of the ways that you're a good tenant. Your boss would be another good choice. They can attest to good qualities related to your work, such as your timeliness and dependability.

Just remember not to ask people you have a close personal relationship with, like your best friend or your mom. A landlord will probably think that they're biased sources.

Remember: **Being organized up front will help you move fast when it counts.**

2.4

START YOUR SEARCH

We know, we know—we can hear you asking, "When do we start looking at those sweet rentals? When can I start looking for my dream place?!?!" Now. Now is the time.

You've done the work to get ready—you know what you want, you have an approach to evaluate places that might be right for you, and you're ready to move fast once you've found the place that's right for you. You're ready to begin the search.

We founded Dwellsy, and so, of course, we think it's the best tool available for your rental searching. But there are other tools out there. Let's go through the landscape of available tools so you have some sense of what they are and how they work.

THE OG: CRAIGSLIST AND ITS DESCENDANTS

Craigslist is where it all began, more or less, for online rentals, and until a few years ago, it was still where most rentals were found. As recently as 2016, we believe (but to be honest, no one can really know for certain) that Craigslist was responsible for more than 80 percent of rental finds.

Now, much has changed, and it's mostly fraudsters advertising on there. We recommend you simply don't use Craigslist—it's just too dangerous and it's not worth the risk. Full stop.

The most notable descendent of the Craigslist tradition is Facebook Marketplace. Like Craigslist, FB Marketplace is a relatively unstructured and unregulated marketplace that's built to sell your old sofa or shoes, as well as to advertise rentals. As a result, it suffers from many of the challenges that Craigslist faced back when it was a functional marketplace for rentals. However, FB Marketplace never really caught on for rentals, so the rental inventory tends to be older, and there aren't many listings worth your time. Plus, there's a significant fraud risk, so if you give it a try, please be very, very careful.

THE PAID, LANDLORD-SUPPORTED ADVERTISING PLATFORMS: ZILLOW, APARTMENTS.COM, REDFIN, AND MORE

A lot of the rental search engines you probably hear about the most are the ones we call "pay to play." You'll recognize familiar names in this category, like Zillow and Apartments.com.

We call them "pay to play" because landlords and property managers pay to list on these sites. In most cases, virtually all of the listings on these sites are paid placements, so you're just seeing a minority of rentals—only those from landlords who are willing to pay to list their properties.

Most landlords (we estimate about 85 percent) are not willing to pay to list under any circumstances, so these sites miss out on most listings.

The advertisers on these sites also pay to have their listings appear higher up in the search results, even above listings that meet more of your criteria. That gums up your search and makes for a frustrating experience.

That said, depending on who you are and what you're looking for, these might be the kind of sites that work best for you.

They typically list lots of apartments in larger apartment communities but relatively few single-family rentals, condos, and small apartment buildings, which are the majority of rentals in the United States.

DWELLSY IS DIFFERENT

Dwellsy doesn't fit into either of these categories, so we're giving it a section all to itself. We know we're a little biased. But we don't think people should have to pick between the two options listed above.

Dwellsy is the first rental-listing service whose principal customers are the renters. With the old, pay-to-play rental-listing services, the landlord is the customer and the renter is, in effect, the product that's being sold to the landlord.

We're not kidding. When you click to inquire about a property on one of those sites, the site often gets paid $15 or $20 by the landlord. They're literally selling your inquiry to the landlord.

At Dwellsy, it's different. You, the renter, are the customer. We don't sell you to anyone. We're here to serve you.

For landlords, it's free to list on Dwellsy so that we can bring renters the most inventory. Plus, because our inventory of available rentals is so extensive, we can do things like remove all the duplicates and expired listings, which others don't do. (Ahem. Maybe someone should talk to those other folks about that.)

Plus, all of us at Dwellsy are hypervigilant about fraud—so much so that we are the only listing service to offer a fraud-free guarantee.

So, while we certainly recommend you use Dwellsy, the top-tier listing services that might be of use and are reputable are as follows:

- ApartmentGuide (Redfin)
- Apartment List
- Apartments.com (CoStar)
- Dwellsy
- ForRent.com (CoStar)
- HotPads (Zillow)
- Redfin
- Rent.com (Redfin)
- StreetEasy (Zillow)
- Trulia (Zillow)
- Zillow
- Zumper

Remember: Where you search matters. Use rental search tools that are built to help you, not ones that are full of scammers or paid placements.

2.5

THE MOST IMPORTANT RULE OF THE SEARCH

We've mentioned this a bunch of times already, but we're really going to hammer it home here because of how important it is: when it comes to getting the rental you want, you *must* be first.

That means you must be the first to inquire. First to apply. First to pay the deposit when the application is approved.

Why is it so important to be first?

Many renters hear "application" and think of rentals as if they're college applications or other kinds of processes where an application window opens, applications are received, and then the "best" candidate is picked.

Perhaps it used to be that way in the United States, but over time, a body of law called Fair Housing has been established to protect all renters from bias in the rental search. There's a ton of depth and complexity to that law (check out Section 1.9), but there's one mammoth change that it brought about in rentals that impacts your search.

For a landlord to avoid the risk of picking a renter for any reason that would be in violation of Fair Housing laws, one of the safest things they can do is process everything they receive in the order it is received.

So, as a result, landlords mostly respond to inquiries in the order they're received. Then, they submit applications for review in the order they're received. Then, they sign leases with the first approved renter who pays.

HOW MUCH DOES BEING FIRST MATTER?

If you're looking to rent a single-family home, a unique condo, or a unit in a small building, being first is the whole ball game. There's only one of each of these, and there can be intense competition for them.

The rule of thumb we've always lived by is that if you're the first to see a place, you have about a fifty-fifty chance of getting it, provided you move quickly at each step from there on.

If you're the fifth person to see a place, your odds are 5 percent or less.

That's right, your odds of getting the place drop by ten times—from 50 percent to 5 percent—just by being fifth versus first. And the difference between first and fifth is sometimes just a few minutes.

It matters less with big apartment communities, particularly if you're less fussy about which unit you're going to rent in the community. These places tend to always have available apartments, the units are somewhat interchangeable, and they price them as close to market rent as possible, so very few deals are available. As a result, they tend to move a little more slowly, and you usually don't need to move as quickly.

But most folks aren't looking to live in those places—they account for only about 15 percent of rentals in the United States.

For the other 85 percent of rentals—and probably the one you're looking for—you need to be first. So how do you do that?

We won't lie: in today's rental market, where available rentals get snatched minutes or hours after they're posted, it's tough. There are strategies, however.

- **Set instant alerts.** "Instant" is the key word here. You want to see relevant rentals as soon as they're posted, not hours after in a daily summary email that some sites send. Dwellsy has its own instant alerts: it's a part of our Dwellsy Edge product. You can sign up at edge.dwellsy.com.

- **Keep your listings organized.** You don't want to be scrambling around, trying to figure out where you've seen a certain listing or if you've sent out an inquiry already. Time is of the essence here, so we want to waste as little of it as possible. Make sure you keep your favorite listings organized in some way, whether that's through a "favorites" feature (like Dwellsy's) or a spreadsheet.
- **Try several rental sites.** Not all sites will have the same listings, so you'll want to cover as much ground as possible. Make sure you're checking as many sites as you can, as regularly as you can, and that you have as many alerts on as possible. If your area has a local site, like NYC's StreetEasy, so much the better.
- **Be flexible with the timing of your tour.** Clear your schedule as much as possible so that you can tour whenever the landlord wants. We know it's tough to schedule around work and life commitments, but to whatever extent you can, it's worth doing. That way, you'll be among the first to see the place.
- **Try several different methods of communication.** If your landlord doesn't indicate a particular preference on the listing, try all of the methods of communication listed, whether text, call, email, carrier pigeon, or smoke signal. Don't overdo it and spam them endlessly, but your interest will certainly be clear if you try every avenue they offer you.
- **Have your documents ready.** We'll say this again later in more detail, but you can usually apply for a rental right after you tour it, so you'll want to bring your documents with you. In Section 2.3, we went over the documents you need; this is just another heads-up.

Remember: We can't say it enough: be first!

2.6

SUBMIT A WINNING INQUIRY

Once you've picked the rental search engine(s) that make sense for you and found a few rentals that appeal to you, you'll want to start getting in touch with landlords to express your interest and set up tours. As we've explained, speed is key, so don't hesitate to get started.

Here are a few tips for you to keep in mind when you first reach out to a potential landlord:

- **Be polite and considerate.** Remember, first impressions count! You'll definitely want to be courteous in your initial email to heighten your chances of getting the apartment. Your landlord will want to rent to a tenant who is easy to get along with, so it's best to start modeling that right away. It's also just nice to be nice, isn't it?
- **Use professional language.** It's best to drop the chatspeak when you're contacting a potential landlord. Using slang like "LOL" and shortcuts like "u" for "you" in writing might make you

come off as immature. In order to make sure that you appear as professional as possible, proofread your emails and/or use the templates that Dwellsy provides. You can have a friend double-check your inquiry if you feel unsure of yourself. Similarly, if you're on the phone with a landlord, be sure to use a kind and courteous tone of voice and keep your language professional. It can help to prepare a short script—especially if you don't like phone calls.

- **Show that you've read the listing.** Landlords get pretty frustrated answering questions that they've already answered in the listing. And as many as 50 percent of questions asked by potential renters fit this description. Simply by reading the listing, you can let the landlord know you've got your act together. There is no sense in missing out on that opportunity. Read the listing and see if your questions are already answered before asking them.
- **Keep it short and sweet.** You probably have a lot of questions about the listing that your landlord put up, but don't worry—you can ask those later. For now, you just want to establish contact between yourself and the landlord so that you can set up a meeting. Being clear and to the point will make you look like a more attractive tenant.
- **Keep an eye on your phone/email and respond promptly.** Nothing sucks more than missing that call about the place you have to have, right? Timing is the key to getting into a rental, so be sure not to miss any emails from a potential landlord. Be prompt in your replies and be sure that you're on top of every possible opportunity! You got this.

Why stop there, though? When you're super interested in a place, you should really go after it, and the right place doesn't come along every day. So . . .

INQUIRE VIA EMAIL AND PHONE

Landlord preferences vary widely, but some landlords regard phone calls as a higher-quality "lead" and answer those first. Others prefer email and are more likely to respond to those inquiries.

For most rentals, both a phone number and a means for digital inquiry (email or otherwise) are provided, and we recommend using both. That's right, you should both call *and* email the landlord.

Is this duplicative? Yes, from your perspective. However, from the landlord's perspective, they are likely to see only one of your inquiries. Your phone call might be the first they receive, but the email might be the tenth. Because the landlord is only really focused on the first handful of inquiries, using multiple methods of contact gives you two shots at being first.

If they do see both the phone call and the email inquiry, that tells them that you're really interested and that you have your act together to do both. Not a bad message to send the landlord. Make sure you read the listing closely before you do this, however—some landlords will indicate how they would like to be contacted.

BOOK THE SOONEST AVAILABLE APPOINTMENT

Regardless of whether you get in touch with the landlord via phone, email, text, or any other mechanism, ask any questions you may have about the property, and then—and this is important—book an appointment to see the property at the earliest possible date.

You want the *first* showing. Not the second showing or third showing. Not a week from next Wednesday. You have to assume that whoever sees it before you will submit an application or give a deposit on the spot—particularly if it's a great place.

Jonas once lost an apartment to two women with a briefcase full of cash who paid six months' rent up front as he was showing up for a tour. If he'd been there an hour earlier, he would have locked in the place instead.

Don't be Jonas. Book the very first showing the landlord makes available. Be up-front, let the landlord know you're serious, and make an effort to accommodate their schedule to see the place as soon as possible.

Remember: Strike a good balance between persistence and politeness, and you'll be fine.

2.7

TOUR LIKE A PRO

You've gotten in touch with a few different landlords about some promising rentals. Now it's time to actually see those places! This is your chance to get a close, personal look at your future home. Of course, you'll want to use this time wisely and find out everything you want to know. We're here to help with our expert tips on touring an apartment like a pro.

QUESTIONS TO ASK THE LANDLORD

Sometimes, the key to success is just to ask the right questions. Touring an apartment is one of those times. There are some things you can't be certain of until you've asked the landlord, and this is your first chance to do so in person.

Like everything else about the rental hunt, these questions should be tailored to your needs. We've just listed a few of the most common concerns people have when it comes to renting.

- **"How do I pay rent?"** Some landlords still prefer a handwritten check above all else. However, there might also be a way you can pay your rent online. While this looks like a more convenient option at first, some rent-collecting systems actually charge fees. Obviously, it's best to know this ahead of time so you can budget for the full rental payment, including additional fees.

- **"What's the parking situation?"** This one's important for any car owner. If you're living in a city and a parking space isn't included in your rent, you'll want to make sure there's consistent room for you to park on the street. There are also properties where you can have a parking space for a fee. This is something you'll want to consider ahead of time.
- **"Do you require renters insurance?"** Generally, we at Dwellsy think it's always a good idea to get renters insurance, just in case of disaster. But putting aside our own opinion, some leases actually require it. It's something you'll want to get sorted ahead of time, especially because it's yet another thing you'll have to budget for. Be sure to ask the landlord so you understand exactly what is required to enable you to sign the lease. Check out Section 4.2 for more on renters insurance.
- **"How do I report a maintenance problem if one comes up?"** Even when a maintenance issue is minor, it can be frustrating to wait for it to be fixed. It's important to understand exactly how to report a maintenance issue, whether that's through a call, an online portal, or something else. Your landlord should also be able to give you a general timeline of how long it takes to fix smaller problems.
- **"Are there any specific restrictions in place that I should know about?"** Sometimes, there are things in the lease agreement that you might not see coming until you read the fine print of your lease. For instance, you might only be able to have a certain number of guests in your rental at one time. Or you might not be able to have a grill on your balcony. Or your landlord has a rule about what can and can't be altered within the apartment. Knowing about these restrictions ahead of time will help you avoid any unpleasant surprises later, especially if any of them conflict with your lifestyle.

QUESTIONS TO ASK YOURSELF

As you tour the property, there are a few key things you can check out around the building. We've split them into the different parts of the tour so that it's easy for you to keep certain questions in mind.

The Outside

- **How does the landscaping look?** It doesn't have to be stunning, but at least check to see if it's well maintained. This is the first sign that someone cares about the property and is looking after it carefully and consistently. Good landscaping often means there's a good chance the rest of the building looks the same.
- **How does the exterior of the building look?** Is the paint peeling or fresh? Are the windows clean or dirty? Are the bricks crumbling or straight-edged? The care put into the building's general appearance will probably be reflected in your rental unit, now and in the future. You want to rent from someone who cares about what the place looks like.
- **What does the signage look like on the doors and in the hallways of the building?** What tone does it set? Is it direct, clear, and professional? That's what you want. Muddled directions might mean muddled management, and you don't want that.

The Inside

- **How clean and neat are the common areas?** Is the floor swept or dirty? If there's a common area with seating, is the furniture clean?
- **Is the carpet/linoleum well maintained, both in common areas and in the unit?** Are there any stains, crumples, cracks, or tiles poking up?
- **How's the smell in the building and the apartment?** A bad odor is a bad sign. Maybe it's just a minor thing, like someone's cooking or someone's pet, but it could also be a sign of mildew. Be sure to ask your landlord about any unpleasant smells so that you can be sure they're not a constant problem.

- **Is the unit you're touring occupied or unoccupied?** If someone's living in the apartment, you don't want to blame the landlord for someone's mess. It might be a little harder to get an accurate picture of the apartment if it's occupied—although if it's obvious that it's not in good condition, that's definitely something you can mention to the landlord.
- **If it's unoccupied, though, everything should be clean and in tip-top shape.** All repairs should have been made, and things should be basically ready to go. If something isn't ready to go, you can expect a good property manager to tell you that they're already dealing with an issue. Ideally, this is the condition you want to see the apartment in.
- **Is the landlord being clear about what needs to be fixed (if anything)?** If all of the maintenance items haven't been taken care of, pay attention to whether you have to bring them up yourself or whether the landlord points them out. This will show that the landlord is observant and isn't trying to hide anything.
- **Are there any signs of mold, mildew, or infestation?** Mold and mildew could be anywhere, but you want to be particularly careful to check wet places, like around sinks, in bathrooms, and near and in washer/dryers. If you notice mold or mildew, be sure to speak up and ask about it. You want to make sure that you're not moving into a rental that already has those problems. The same goes if you see evidence of a critter infestation, like holes and chewed edges in walls, cupboards, and baseboards. Asking questions right off the bat could prevent issues later.

Key Things to Check Yourself

As you're walking around the rental unit, there are a few questions you can ask yourself about how well maintained the place is. Again, we've broken this section down into rooms so that it's easy for you to refer to.

General:

- Do the locks work, and are the doors secure?

- Do the windows open and shut without issue?
- How's the cell-phone service?
- Are there smoke detectors?
- Do the outlets work? Are there enough of them? Are they conveniently placed?
- If there are laundry machines, do they look clean and functional?

Kitchen:

- Do the faucets work? How's the water pressure?
- How's the storage space in the cabinets? Is there any evidence of pests? (You'd be surprised by what you can find and how much heartache you can save yourself by opening a few floor-level cabinets.)
- Do the appliances look like they're in good working order? The stove, the microwave, the dishwasher, the refrigerator/freezer?

Bedrooms:

- Is there a closet? How's the storage space?
- If there's a ceiling fan, does it work?
- Does the built-in lighting work?
- Is there room for your bed? What about your dresser, or a desk if you have one?

Bathrooms:

- Do the faucets work?
- Does the toilet flush well?
- Does the shower work? How's the water pressure? Is the head mounted firmly into the wall? Does the water drain correctly?

Living Room:

- How does the sound travel through the walls? If someone is standing in the next room over, close to the wall, can you hear them? Ask about the materials used in the building's structure—concrete in particular is good for keeping noise out. If you can come at a few different times of the day to check for the noise levels, you should.

WHAT CAN YOU ASK FOR?

Here are a few reasonable things the landlord might be willing to implement, should you notice issues when you tour:

- New paint, if necessary
- New carpet, if necessary
- New appliances, if necessary
- Ionizing treatment to eliminate odors from pets or smoking
- A thorough cleaning

To ensure you get the changes you've agreed upon, ask for any promises the landlord makes in writing.

CHECKING OUT THE NEIGHBORHOOD

A rental isn't just the apartment and its building—it's the surrounding area, too. While you're in the neighborhood, why not scope out the situation? You can walk around a bit and see if it feels clean, safe, and friendly. If you've got time for a bite, why not see if the local food is any good? Bonus points for coming back after dark to see how it feels to you then. Hopefully, you like the neighborhood just as much as you like the home or apartment itself. Here are a few questions to consider:

- Is the neighborhood bustling or quiet? (Another thing to consider when you're thinking about how much noise you'll hear in your apartment.)
- Is it clean or dirty?
- How's the food scene? Are there restaurants you like nearby?
- Are there green spaces nearby?

- How close is the nearest grocery store? Hopefully there are a few. What about a convenience store or corner shop?
- Is the community friendly? Do you see evidence of community social or cultural events?

Once you've toured an apartment or house and you're sure that you'd want to rent there, the next step is to apply. Hopefully, you can apply immediately after the apartment tour, so be sure to look over our next section on applications before you go to any apartment tours.

Remember: If you have any questions, ask your landlord—that's why they're there. You can also ask someone in the building how they like living there.

2.8

NAIL THE APPLICATION

After searching and touring, you've probably come across a few apartments you'd like to rent. That's great! Get started on your application process right away.

BE PROACTIVE AND GET IN FIRST

Have we mentioned that you should submit the first application? You want to be the first application in the pile, if at all possible. Landlords often take the first applicant who fits their needs. Every day that a rental unit sits empty costs a landlord money, so if they find a good tenant, they're not going to wait to see if a better one comes along.

So how do you make sure you get in first? When you tour, come prepared. You'll often be able to apply for the rental you're touring right then and there while you're with the agent or landlord in the building. If you have the necessary documents and information, you can ensure that you waste no time getting your application in.

HOW TO PUT TOGETHER A STELLAR APPLICATION

So how do you put together the best application possible? Here are our best tips to ensure that your application presents you as an amazing tenant.

Write a Good Cover Letter (If Accepted)

In certain circumstances, there's an opportunity to write a cover letter in which you can tell your story. It's a part of a rental application that feels a little like a job application. A good cover letter should show your enthusiasm for a rental.

In your letter, you can explain things that might not come through in the other sections of your application, such as the reasons why you like the rental and how you plan to be a good tenant. We know writing cover letters isn't anyone's idea of a good time, but at least it's a useful opportunity to round out your application. It's great to have one ready in advance, just in case, so you can cut and paste with a little customization about the rental.

If You Have Pets, Be Up-Front About It

We know you might dread having to discuss your pet with a landlord. And it's true: landlords usually don't like pets. But, as with your credit score, your best shot is to be straightforward and honest about your pet. Landlords will want to rent to a tenant who tackles problems ahead of time instead of avoiding them, and this is a chance to show you're capable of that.

If it's not clear that your landlord will welcome your pet, you can offer to let them meet your pet ahead of time so they can see how well behaved and quiet it is. (Note: better make sure your pet actually is well behaved and quiet before you take this route!) You can also include a photo of your pet. Be sure to offer any registration and training certificates your pet may have earned to show that their good behavior is endorsed by an outside source. These things may make a landlord more willing to rent to you and your furry friend.

Be Polite and Courteous

We know we've really been hammering home politeness. We're going to say it again, though: no matter what, be as polite and courteous as you can. The last person a landlord wants to rent to is someone who's unpleasant to deal with.

If you rent from them, the two of you will be in a professional relationship. You want to behave according to those expectations. Even if the landlord's responses are curt or they seem to take a while to respond, do your best to be as polite as you would be to a coworker.

Be Communicative Throughout the Process

Keep in touch with your potential landlord about your application. If a landlord asks for additional documents, make sure to send the information as promptly as you can. And check to make sure that the documents were received. If you've just had a big life change that affects your income, be open and honest about it. Generally, you want to keep a potential landlord in the know about anything that affects you as a tenant.

Be Flexible

When it comes to landing a rental, sometimes a little flexibility is the key. We've devoted a section to negotiating your lease (Section 2.10) because it's an important tool to have in your toolbox. Before you apply, though, think through where you're willing to make concessions. Can you move in a little early? Pay a slightly higher security deposit? Provide a guarantor? These are all things that can make or break your chances with a landlord, so be ready to adapt if you have to.

Follow Up

If you don't hear about an application after a day or two, it's good practice to follow up. Maybe one of your emails didn't go through or a landlord's request for documents landed in your spam. It would suck for something like that to stop you from landing an amazing home, right? So if it's been a while, check in.

When you apply, you can always ask the landlord when they expect to reach a decision. That way, you'll know when to reach out to them, and you won't appear pushy.

Remember: Clarity, communication, and honesty are your keys to a strong application. Make sure you move fast and get your application in quickly.

2.9

READ YOUR LEASE

Ah, the lease. An excruciating legal document—small print, written by lawyers, with a crazy number of terms in it.

We've seen leases that are one page long (scary!), and we've seen them running as long as eighty-five pages (also scary!). They can be brutal to read.

A lease is, however, a formal, enforceable contract you are signing, and a big one because it concerns your home. For most of us, this is the biggest expense in our budgets and one of the biggest commitments we take on.

You need to read your lease before you sign it. And we should all eat our broccoli, too, but who does it, right? This one you actually really need to do, though. It's a big commitment, and it's got the potential to be important to your life in this new place, so do whatever you need to do to get ready and sit down and read it as closely and thoroughly as you can.

There are an infinite variety of leases, so we can't tell you how to read your specific one, and we're not attorneys, so we can't give you legal counsel. We can help you think about what to look for, however, so here are the main things you need to make sure you understand after reading your lease.

HOW MUCH DO YOU HAVE TO PAY?

You need to make sure that you see the rental price listed in the lease. It should be very clearly identified.

Just as, or perhaps even more, important are the other potential costs that may be included in your lease, such as a security deposit, smoking fees, renters insurance, pet fees, parking fees, utilities that you're responsible for, storage costs, late fees, and others.

Look for all the costs that you'll have to pay and add them up. Total monthly costs are often more than rent alone, but these additional costs are sometimes ignored and too often a surprise for new renters. If you're already stretching to afford the rent on your place and find out you have to pay 20 percent more because of additional fees, these costs might put that new place out of your reach. It's better to know that before you sign the lease than to discover after signing or even moving in that the monthly costs are too much for your budget.

HOW DO YOU PAY YOUR RENT AND FEES?

Landlords can be funny about how they want to get paid. Some are old-school and want a check, or in some cases, cash (make sure you get a receipt!). Some are all about modern conveniences and would like you to pay online through a portal they've set up. Some want you to pay via Zelle or Venmo (be careful!). It's good to know in advance so you can be ready and pay promptly.

HOW LONG IS YOUR LEASE?

The official language is usually "lease term," and in the United States it's usually twelve months, but increasingly that's not always the case.

It's quite common to find thirteen- or fourteen-month leases, and there's an increasing trend to offer sixteen- or eighteen-month leases as well.

Often, landlords will try to avoid having a lease end in the winter (remember, rent is often lower in the winter), so if you're signing a lease in the winter months, be particularly aware of the potential for a nontraditional lease length.

Is There an Acceleration Clause?

Sometimes, a landlord will be thinking about selling their place, and they may have a clause in the lease that allows them to end your lease early if they sell the place. If this clause is there, you should take it as a warning that your landlord is likely to sell your place and that you're likely to be asked to move before the end of your lease.

HOW MANY PEOPLE CAN LIVE IN YOUR PLACE?

There is often a legal limit or landlord-imposed cap on the number of people who can live in a rental. This should be specified in the lease.

CAN YOU HAVE A PET?

Whether or not you have a pet now, it's good to know whether the lease permits having a pet because you might want to get one later.

WHAT'S THE LANDLORD'S RIGHT OF ENTRY?

All landlords have the right to get into their rentals under certain circumstances. Understanding the landlord's rights in this case will help you maintain peace with them. Does the lease give them unlimited access to deal with emergencies (which they should probably have, since an emergency can destroy your home)? Does it say that they have to give you twenty-four hours' notice to enter?

WHAT ARE THE COMMUNITY RULES?

When you're living in an apartment community, you're living with other folks, so the lease will often include a set of rules to set standards and expectations to help everyone get along, such as quiet hours, common-area rules, and trash-disposal instructions.

Usually, these are unsurprising, but not always. It's worth reading this section of the lease in some detail to make sure you can live with the house rules and know when you might have trouble with them.

ARE THERE BANNED ACTIVITIES OR SUBSTANCES?

Many leases include clauses that don't allow you to use a rental in certain ways. For example, it's typical not to allow you to run a business from a rental home or apartment, which is usually the city's rule and not the landlord's, but it's included in the lease to protect the landlord.

Increasingly, landlords are including "no smoking" clauses in their leases that allow them to end the lease and impose heavy cleaning costs on the renter if there is smoking in the rental.

Often, there are lease terms that allow the landlord to end the lease if any illegal drugs or substances are used in the rental. In particular, with today's unpredictable legal environment around substances like marijuana, it's great to know such terms before you sign.

There are also usually clauses about making excessive noise or other activities that might be a nuisance to your neighbors. Again, you should review these rules so you can decide if this is the place that suits your needs and lifestyle.

CAN YOU SUBLET OR LIST YOUR RENTAL ON AIRBNB?

Depending on your place and situation, you might be interested in making a bit of money by renting your place for a night here and there or getting out of the lease early by passing it over to a friend or new renter (a subletter). Your lease will outline whether these activities are allowed by your landlord.

WHAT HAPPENS AT THE END OF YOUR LEASE?

What happens at the end of a lease varies widely, often according to regional norms. In some places, it's typical for leases to just end, with no provision for ongoing residency. In others, it's common for leases to turn into a month-to-month lease after the first twelve months.

You may also have some right of renewal, potentially at a pre-negotiated rent level, which can be highly valuable if you want to stay in your place at the end of the lease.

You should also know how much notice you have to give if you want to move out so that you can plan accordingly. Some leases will allow the landlord to charge a fee if you don't give them enough notice that you are leaving. They typically want to be notified thirty, forty-five, or sixty days before you move out.

HOW DO YOU GET YOUR SECURITY DEPOSIT BACK?

Usually, there will be specific language about security-deposit return and what it means to satisfy the return requirements. This is important to understand from the moment of signing your lease so you can make sure to get your security deposit back at the end.

IS THERE ANYTHING REALLY WEIRD?

We are all the result of our experiences, and your landlord is, too. Some landlords have some pretty funny things in their leases as a result of weird or awful past experiences, so keep an eye out for those.

Have more questions? Your leasing agent or landlord should be able to answer any questions about the lease for you and help you understand it. If you need more help, we have a list of local renters' organizations on the Dwellsy website (Dwellsy.com/blog/renters/rentersorganizations).

And, if neither of those work for you, then talk to a local lawyer who is familiar with residential landlord/tenant law. That said, if the lease is so challenging that you feel the need to talk to a lawyer about it, this probably isn't the right rental for you. The lease is often a sign of how easy or difficult the landlord will be to get along with. Highly complex leases aren't usually a good sign. If the lease is long and super complicated, you might want to think about finding another landlord who's easier to deal with.

Remember: It's one thing to read your lease, but you also need to make sure you *understand* it. If there's something you're confused about, ask your landlord or someone else for help.

2.10

NEGOTIATE YOUR LEASE

Let's say that you're approved for a rental unit or two. Congrats! All of your hard work is paying off, and you should be proud. Your new apartment is closer than ever.

You've read the lease, and you think you understand it. There might be a thing or two in there that you didn't see coming, though. Maybe the rent is a little higher than you expected, or maybe utilities aren't included in your rent when you thought they would be. Not to worry! Now is the time to negotiate your lease.

Yep, that's right—the terms of your lease can be negotiated, just like tons of other situations in life. Not sure how to go about a negotiation? Read on, and we'll help you out.

UNDERSTAND YOUR LEASE

The first step to a successful negotiation is understanding the terms of your lease as described in the prior section. Make note of the terms that you'd like to negotiate.

COMPARE YOUR RENTAL TO OTHERS IN THE AREA

One of the best tools in your negotiation toolbox is research. Take a look around at other rental apartments in the area. Maybe a parking space is free for lots of them, or the rent's a little lower, or there's no pet rent. Being able to bring these facts to the table will make your negotiating position stronger. Your landlord could be more willing to give you something if they know other landlords in the area are doing it.

UNDERSTAND WHAT THE LANDLORD WANTS AND NEEDS

You might know what you want when it comes to changing your lease. Negotiation is a two-way street, though, so you should also know what your landlord wants. Getting to know your landlord will help you out here. What are their biggest concerns? What was their experience with the last tenant of the unit? Are you their only prospective tenant or just one of many?

Smaller landlords will be more worried about vacancies because empty units can cost so much money (recall Section 1.4, where we discussed how landlords make money). They might be more willing to lower your rent for a longer lease or something similar. They also might not have a full maintenance team the way that large property-management companies do. If you're handy, you could trade your skills for something useful to you: utilities, perhaps, or a parking space.

Landlords who own multiple properties or larger rental communities have lots of areas where they can cut prices. They might be able to offer you a lower security deposit, free parking, storage units, or other things. This is all dependent on what you can bring to the table.

Here's a secret tip from us: larger landlords are interested in protecting the "base rent." This is the rent that you pay every month. They want this amount to be as high as it can be. This means that it's easier to ask larger landlords for concessions other than lower regular monthly rent, like free parking, storage space, lower fees, or up-front months of free rent. They might be willing to give more in these areas than on the base rent.

Also, with larger landlords—big companies and/or big communities—you might want to negotiate with them before you get the lease. It can be very hard to change the lease with them, so the timeline of negotiation might be a bit different from the one you're likely to encounter with the majority of smaller landlords.

Let's negotiate!

THE ASK

Before you hit up your landlord to discuss your negotiation, you should know exactly what you want. We know this seems obvious at first, but it's worth it to take some time and really think things through. For example, say you want your security deposit reduced. By how much, exactly? Or say you want utilities to be covered in the rent. Precisely which utilities?

It's a good idea to write down your requests. If you have a written list of things you'd like, you won't forget them when you're actually talking to your landlord. You'll come across as clear and thoughtful during the conversation, too. By expressing your desires in concrete terms, you'll help your landlord understand exactly what you need and how they can help you.

You could ask for things like:

- Lower rent
- Free month or months of rent at the beginning of your lease
- A longer or shorter lease term (maybe ending in the winter?!)
- Free pet rent, parking, gym access, or other amenities
- Some or all utilities paid for by the landlord
- Predictable renewal terms, such as negotiating a maximum rent increase or guarantees that you can renew your lease

But the ask is only half of the conversation. Think about things you can offer, too, in order to make the pot sweeter. You could:

- Help out with maintenance and yard work
- Sign a longer lease—maybe two years instead of one
- Move in earlier
- Pay a higher amount of rent in exchange for free rent up front

By understanding what your landlord wants and needs, you can speak to those desires with what you offer in your negotiation.

THE CONVERSATION

Once you've got everything planned out, the conversation itself should be pretty straightforward, though we know it's often a little nerve-wracking because most of us aren't used to negotiating, and it may even be your first attempt at it.

Here are some of our best tips to help make sure that things go smoothly:

- **Wait until you're approved to negotiate.** If you negotiate before your application has even been approved, you might simply take yourself out of the running right away. If you negotiate after you've been approved, you already know the landlord is excited about you as a tenant. They'll likely be more willing to rearrange your contract a bit to suit you.
- **Be courteous.** Your landlord is a person, too! They deserve your kindness and courtesy during the negotiation process. You're much more likely to get the concessions you're looking for if you're polite to the landlord.
- **Include a "give" with your "ask."** Make sure that when you explain what you want, you also explain what you can give in return. This makes it seem less like you're just asking for something and more like an equal exchange. For instance, if you want your rent to be lower, immediately include the fact that you'll do yard work to compensate.

- **Be ready to back your requests up with evidence if you have to.** If you're asking for something because you've realized that it's something nearby rentals offer, like free parking or a smaller security deposit, make sure you can tell your landlord exactly where you're getting that information. Having solid evidence will make your case stronger.
- **Be reasonable.** Keep your expectations realistic. If the rent is $1,500, and you want to ask for it to be $500, you'll probably end up disappointed. Not sure whether your ask makes sense? Check the local market on Dwellsy to see what other rentals in the area offer.
- **Understand your leverage.** If there were twenty people clamoring to submit applications at the tour, then the landlord can easily move on to another renter. If the place has been available for a little while and the landlord is still looking for a tenant, then you have a better bargaining position.
- **Respect the anchor.** In negotiations, there's a concept known as "anchoring." By advertising a rent for the apartment, the landlord has anchored the negotiation with a starting point on price—the anchor is the starting point for the negotiation. Successful negotiators know that it can be difficult to move the other side off something on which they've anchored, so it often makes sense to focus on other asks and leave the anchor in place. If you really want to go after something on which the landlord is anchored, that's fine, but respect the fact that the landlord may be emotionally invested in that anchor.

THE BACK AND FORTH

Ideally, your landlord will immediately say yes to your request. It's unlikely it will be that simple, though. Your landlord will probably have to think about what you're asking for and talk to someone else before you can reach an agreement. For instance, if you're working with a leasing agent from a large property-management company, they'll probably have to talk to the corporate office.

Be sure to listen to the landlord's response when they get back to you. Take time to consider why they might not agree with your proposal. What do they need that you haven't offered?

There's a good chance your landlord will come back with a few different options you hadn't considered before. You'll have to evaluate them yourself and decide what makes sense for you. You might have to ask yourself: How strongly do I feel about the apartment? Am I still willing to rent on the terms of the original lease? How flexible can I be with my original ask? Is it possible I could concede something more or different?

Remember: you want to live in this apartment and the landlord wants to rent to you. There's a deal to be found somewhere, even if you have to compromise for it. Keep your cool and keep the situation friendly and calm. You're going to end up having that professional relationship with this landlord if you live in their rental unit, so you'll want to start off on the right foot.

The best result of a negotiation is that you end up in a great place at a fair price and with a strong relationship with a good landlord. We all want that, right? Here's hoping you pull it off. We sure think you can.

Once you have a deal in place, get the revised lease and read it through to confirm the changes are there—and then it's time to move on to the final step!

Remember: Negotiation is your key to making your rental experience what you want it to be. Use it thoughtfully.

2.11

PAY THE LANDLORD

Exciting times! You've done the hard work to find your next home, you know what's in the lease, and you've negotiated a deal that both you and your landlord can agree on.

If you remember back to Section 1.7, you'll recall that the various up-front payments are all outlined there in detail in the context of budgeting for your new place.

Now, let's talk about when you should expect to have to pay money and—importantly for your safety—when you shouldn't!

TIMING

Here's what a typical schedule looks like for payments and amounts, beginning from the moment you decide you want a place:

Timing	Expense Type	Expense Amount	Refundable?
Day 1	Application Fee	$35–60 per application	No
Day 2–3	Holding Deposit	($100 to 25 percent of the rent)	Yes, if you rent the place

Timing	Expense Type	Expense Amount	Refundable?
Day 3–5	First and Last Month's Rent OR First Month's Rent and Security Deposit	Usually two months' rent	Security deposit is, if there is no damage.
Day 3–5	Other: Pet Deposit, Move-In Fees	Varies widely	Deposits: Yes Fees: No

As you can see from the chart, once your application is approved, the landlord expects payment of other up-front costs pretty quickly, so it's best to have your budgeted amount set aside and ready to go when you're looking.

Remember, speed matters in this process, and you want to be first. If you're the first application that's submitted and approved, but you take your time getting the holding deposit in, there's a chance that the second or third application could sneak past you and lock down the place before you can.

That said, you need to balance speed with safety and your own risk of losing big money.

If you have done the following, then you should be in pretty good shape from a safety standpoint, so you can afford to move quickly with payments:

1. Found the listing on a reputable site like Dwellsy
2. Met the landlord or their representative in person
3. Toured the inside of the rental
4. Found a normal online presence from the landlord or their representative

If some or all of the above do not apply to your search, then you should be a little suspect about handing over money and be willing to move more slowly, even if it means losing the place. It's better to lose the place and find another rather than lose your hard-earned savings!

METHOD OF PAYMENT

With most landlords, the method of payment will be fairly typical and is usually as follows, broken down by the different types of property manager. "Professionally managed" properties refer to those either managed by a corporate owner/operator or a third-party property manager (covered in Section 1.2).

Professionally Managed Properties

Fee	Typical Payment Types
Application Fee	Credit card, check, or money order
Holding Deposit	Credit card or check
First/Last/Security Deposit	Check, electronic funds transfer, or wire

Individual Landlords

Fee	Typical Payment Types
Application Fee	Credit card, check, cash, or Venmo/Zelle
Holding Deposit	Check or Venmo/Zelle
First/Last/Security Deposit	Check, electronic funds transfer, wire, or Venmo/Zelle

Here's where you need to be really careful. Venmo and Zelle (and cash, of course) are one-way payment mechanisms that are nearly impossible to reverse. If asked to provide payment via these mechanisms, you need to be *very* sure you're dealing with a legit landlord.

Here at Dwellsy, we advise every renter to avoid tools like Venmo and Zelle for any up-front payments. The application fee, however, is a lower-cost item (so, a lower risk—losing $35 isn't the crisis that losing $3,500 is), and if you'd like to pay for month two of rent and beyond via those tools, that's much safer. Most of the risk of scammers is with the payments before you've occupied your new home, so we would strongly recommend avoiding those tools until you're living in the place.

If the "landlord" will only accept payment via those risky mechanisms, be careful! Again, check out Section 1.5 to understand what you should be doing to stay safe in this process, and make sure your funds are going to pay for your new home and not lining some scammer's pockets.

Remember: You'll want to be able to pay your landlord those up-front costs right when you're asked for them, so make sure you have that money set aside.

Section 3
YOUR UNIQUE RENTAL SITUATION

Every single one of us is unique. You're unique. Hannah's unique. Jonas is unique. When each of us sets out to find a place, each of our rental searches differs—and that means we all bump into some unique and tricky situations.

The previous section covered the typical search for a place from start to finish. This section aims to help you through a variety of circumstances that might make your search unique.

Is your pet unique? Sure it is! Is your roommate unique? Definitely. Is your shoe collection unique? Yes, without a doubt. Do you have to find a place in a hurry? Do you need a more unusual type of property?

Each one of these considerations can complicate the rental-search process. We'll try to keep it as simple as possible but will dive into the details where necessary in this section. If you can't find answers to your unique questions here, write to us (RenterQs@Dwellsy.com) and let us know, and we'd be happy to address your questions on our blog at Dwellsy.com/blog/RenterQs.

3.1

HOW TO FIND A HOME FOR YOUR FURRY FRIENDS

It can be hard to find a place to rent if you have a pet. We know that it's frustrating to be turned away by landlord after landlord just for wanting to have your furry friend around, and we're here to help you out. In this section, we'll talk about exactly why landlords don't like pets and what you can do to combat their concerns. We'll also talk about pet-friendly housing and its pros and cons. Then, we'll go over different kinds of legal classifications for your pets that might be important under housing law.

WHY DON'T LANDLORDS LIKE PETS?

So you want to show your landlord that you're capable of having a pet and being a responsible tenant. First, you'll need to understand exactly why landlords don't like pets in the first place. Then, we can talk about how to show them that you'll take care of their concerns. Let's talk about a few of the reasons that landlords generally don't like having pets in their rental units.

Pets Can Damage Rentals

One of the major reasons landlords don't like pets is because they can damage their properties. Your cat might be adorable most of the time, but what if she decides that your bedroom's wallpaper is her new scratching post? We know your puppy is the cutest thing in the world—until he decides that the brand-new carpet is the best place to "mark his territory."

There's no doubt about it: having a pet increases the potential for damage to your rental. You might be a really good pet owner, and your pet might be obedient and well behaved, but there are no guarantees. If your pet damages the rental, your landlord will have to find time and potentially money to schedule someone to come in and fix it. This takes up their time and energy, even if you're the one footing the bill.

Your landlord is always looking for ways to minimize the risk of damage to their rental. If they've got a pile of applications, and they're choosing between a pet owner and someone without a pet, picking the person without the pet can be an easy choice.

Pets Can Have an Odor

You've probably adjusted to your pet's natural odor after living with them for a while. Other people might not feel neutral about it, however. Your pet's odor might bother your neighbors. Pet odor can also linger long after you've moved out, meaning that the landlord will have to find ways to get rid of it even after you're gone. This could impact how easy it will be to rent the place out to the next tenant.

Pets Can Annoy Neighbors

Aside from their odor, there are a few other ways your pet might bother your neighbors. To people who don't own pets, even quiet animal noises can seem loud or annoying. The last thing a landlord wants to do is spend time dealing with complaints between two tenants. They'll want to rent to someone who isn't likely to cause noise complaints, and your pet might not count in your favor here.

Pets Could Injure Someone

If your pet injures someone, it's possible your landlord will be at risk for the medical bills. Maybe you're thinking, "Whoa, my pet would never hurt anyone!" Of course, maybe they wouldn't. But a potential landlord doesn't know your pet as well as you do, so they'll still consider them a risk. It could be as simple as your dog getting overexcited while playing with a child from the apartment next door. Or maybe your cat is getting a little nippy in their old age.

No matter what, your landlord is going to want to lower the risk of someone being injured on their property. So in order to avoid all of these potential problems, it makes sense for landlords to be somewhat reluctant to rent to pet owners.

HOW TO SHOW YOUR LANDLORD THAT YOU'RE A RESPONSIBLE PET OWNER

If you're a responsible pet owner with a well-behaved pet, you probably feel like you could take care of these concerns if a landlord would give you a chance. The good news is there are ways to show your landlord that you and your pet won't cause any trouble as tenants.

Open a Dialogue

You understand some of the general reasons why landlords might not want to rent to pet owners. Now, you can go to your landlord and ask what their specific concerns are. That way, you can tackle those issues head-on. This will demonstrate to your landlord that you're communicative and willing to tackle problems before they grow into larger issues.

So, how do you tackle specific issues? Here are some examples: Your landlord is worried about noise? Great, you can bring in reference letters from former landlords stating that your pet is quiet. Your landlord is worried about your large dog getting out of control? Perfect, you can bring in training certificates to show that your dog is obedient and well behaved. Be specific and get your proof from an objective source, and you can't go wrong.

Introduce Your Landlord to Your Pet

Offer to bring your pet in to meet your landlord so that the two can get acquainted. If your landlord sees that your pet is quiet and well behaved, it could help your case. The downside of this is that if your pet is loud and aggressive, it could make things worse. You'll want to be sure that your pet consistently behaves well in the company of others before you suggest a meeting with your landlord.

Show Your Landlord Any Training Certificates Your Pet Has Earned

It can be helpful to show your landlord evidence from an objective authority that your pet is well trained. If you have any training certificates from a professional organization, they could help reassure your landlord. Your landlord won't just have to take your word that your animal is obedient.

Ask Former Landlords for Reference Letters

That's right—you can get reference letters for your pet. A letter from a former landlord testifying that your pet is quiet and well behaved could give you a serious boost in credibility. Your current landlord will appreciate hearing from someone who has been in their shoes and decided to trust you as a pet owner. Obviously, make sure you ask a landlord who really believes that your pet is well behaved. You don't want to show your new landlord a negative letter!

Get Some Extra Insurance

Sometimes, getting your landlord to accept your pet is as simple as getting some extra insurance coverage to eliminate any risk that they may face. There are some renters-insurance programs that will allow you to add coverage for pet risk. Having that in place will send the message to the landlord that you understand their concerns and you're willing to take action to make sure your pet is welcome.

PET RENT, PET DEPOSITS, AND PET FEES

If you have a pet, your landlord might ask you to pay "pet rent," a "pet deposit," or a "pet fee." You can also offer these things during negotiations if your landlord is reluctant to rent to a pet owner. Here's a list of these different terms and their definitions:

- **Pet rent** is a recurring addition to your rent, so it's paid monthly and is not refundable.
- A **pet deposit** is a one-time, refundable deposit paid at the beginning of your tenancy. You'll get it back in full at the end of your lease if your pet causes no damage to the rental.
- A **pet fee** is nonrefundable. It can be either one-time or monthly, depending on your location and your landlord.

Of course, whatever your landlord ends up charging you, it will be written in your lease. Check your local laws to see what they have to say about pet rent and other such charges. In some states, it's legal, and in others, it's illegal. You'll want to know what the situation is before you start looking for an apartment.

PET-FRIENDLY RENTALS

Maybe you don't want to fight an uphill battle when it comes to renting with your pet. That's totally understandable. In that case, you'll want to consider pet-friendly rentals. These are rental buildings that cater specifically to the needs of pet owners and their animals.

What Makes Pet-Friendly Apartments Different?

There are two main ways that pet-friendly apartments set themselves apart from normal apartment buildings: amenities and community. Let's talk through both of these to give you a better idea of what you can expect from a pet-friendly apartment.

Amenities

The selection of amenities might be the best part of pet-friendly living. Of course, every apartment building will offer different things, but here is a list of the most common pet-friendly amenities.

- **Bark parks or play areas.** In many pet-friendly apartment complexes, you won't have to walk very far to find an outdoor space for your pet. Many pet-friendly buildings have their own parks or play areas on their property. With a play space so close, you can find more time to hang out with your furry friend.
- **Pet walking.** When you're super busy, it can be hard to find time to walk your pet. This can make things difficult for you and your animal, especially if you have a dog breed that needs exercise every day to stay healthy. Lots of pet-friendly apartments offer on-site dog-walking services (at an additional cost) to help you out. If you use this type of service, you'll be able to schedule regular walks with a trusted walker so that you can be certain your furry friend is getting enough exercise.
- **Pet sitting.** Having a pet can make it difficult to take time away from your home. You might end up constantly worried about whether you'll get home in time to feed them or whether they're getting into some kind of mischief. That's why some pet-friendly communities offer pet-sitting services (again, at an additional cost). If you want to take a vacation or visit family, or if you need to be away on business, a trusted pet sitter will take care of your animal. By making use of this amenity, you can be certain that your pet is in good hands, and you'll worry less about what to do if you have to leave them for an extended period of time.
- **Dentist and vet appointments.** Wouldn't it be nice to have a vet right in your building? Some pet-friendly apartments have pet dentists and vets come in on certain days of the week so that their tenants can schedule regular appointments. This cuts out all of the stress around getting your pet to the vet, from scheduling appointments to transporting your pet to the veterinarian.

- **Pet-washing stations.** If your pet often gets dirty during their walks, you'll love this amenity. This could save you the hassle of having to clean your floor or even your carpet. No one likes muddy paw prints!
- **Treats in the lobby.** This is a simple one, but it's cute. Lots of pet-friendly apartment buildings keep bowls of water and treats in their lobbies. That way, if your pet has been particularly good during a walk, you can reward them straight away. This also shows how welcoming these apartment complexes try to be toward pet owners—it's clear as soon as you walk in.

Pet-Loving Community

Having a good community in your apartment complex can be a huge boost to your quality of life. If you're a pet owner, you might really enjoy being around other pet owners. After all, you'll have something in common with everyone else who lives in your complex. Pet-friendly apartment complexes can offer you this kind of built-in community in a way most other apartment buildings can't.

Of course, you'll have the opportunity to socialize with other pet owners when you're sharing the apartment building's amenities, like any common outdoor areas. But lots of pet-friendly buildings also offer social events for their tenants, like "Yappy Hour" cocktail get-togethers. Whether you need advice about your pet or you just want to be around people who "get it," the community in a pet-friendly building will be there for you.

Even if you're not interested in being super social, there are still benefits to being surrounded by a community of pet owners. Your neighbors will be more understanding of the messes, smells, and noises that come with owning a pet. They might also be more willing to do small favors, like feeding your pet while you're at work. It can be nice to know you're around people who understand the importance of your pet in your life.

Are Pet-Friendly Apartments More Expensive?

Yes, pet-friendly apartments are sometimes more expensive than their non-pet-friendly counterparts. This is because of all of the amenities they offer and because they cater to a specific community. When you take into account all the hassle of finding an apartment that will let you have a pet, maybe the higher rent is worth it to you. It's something to consider.

"Pet Friendly" vs. "Pets Allowed"

It's obvious that "no pets allowed" apartments aren't interested in having pet owners as tenants, but you might still be wondering about "pets allowed" apartments. "Pets allowed" indicates a landlord that's open to pet owners but not as welcoming as a pet-friendly place will be. You're not likely to find any pet amenities here, nor the sense of community in pet-friendly buildings. The landlord is also less likely to be lenient about things like loud noises and smells. If it comes down to a choice between "pet friendly" and "pets allowed," "pet friendly" often wins out for pet owners.

What Kinds of Pets Are Allowed in a Pet-Friendly Apartment?

Not all kinds of pets will be welcome in pet-friendly apartments. The exact kinds of pets allowed in the apartment building will be up to the landlord. There might be some restrictions around breed, weight, number of pets, and other characteristics. Like other landlords, pet-friendly landlords are concerned about damage to their rental units, and any restrictions they impose will probably aim to minimize damage, which may or may not align with what you believe. (Don't even get us started on whether breed restrictions make sense!) In other cases, a landlord might impose restrictions for the sake of tenants already living in the building, or they may just have personal preferences.

If your pet doesn't fit a pet-friendly building's requirements, you should still reach out to the landlord and try negotiating. Who knows; maybe they'll make an exception for you! They're pet friendly, after all. If you can provide evidence that your animal is well trained, they might just give you and your buddy a shot.

Another note: if you're moving states, remember to check if your pet is legal in your new state. (For instance, keeping ferrets and hedgehogs as pets is illegal in the state of California.)

Which Breeds Are Most Likely to Be Restricted and Why?

As we've said, landlords often choose to restrict certain dog breeds. They do this not only to minimize damage to their own rentals but also to make their tenants more comfortable. Many people do not want to live in an apartment complex with a dog that they might consider aggressive (whether or not the dog actually is). This also means that the landlord will worry less about somehow becoming responsible for dog-inflicted injuries on their property.

In some cases, the landlord's insurance company will require them to restrict certain dog breeds on their property in order to minimize the damage risk. Of course, if there are city or county bans on a certain dog breed, the landlord will also have to abide by those. That's why we mentioned double-checking that your pet is legal if you plan to move states or even cities.

So what kinds of dog breeds are restricted? It varies depending on the landlord and the location, but there are a few breeds that are more likely to be banned:

- Pit bulls
- Rottweilers
- Bulldogs
- Akitas
- Mastiffs
- Great Danes
- Doberman Pinschers
- Boxers

In addition to breed restrictions, you might also come across height and weight restrictions. Make sure to check whether your pet falls within these.

Want your landlord to grant you an exception to their breed restrictions? Refer back to the part of this section entitled "How to Show Your Landlord That You're a Responsible Pet Owner." A lot of those same tactics will work here. You want to show your landlord that your dog is well behaved and responsible. They might just give you a little leeway if they are able.

SERVICE ANIMALS AND EMOTIONAL-SUPPORT ANIMALS

If you have a service animal or an emotional-support animal (ESA), this section is for you. We'll go over what qualifies a pet as one of these types of animal and what you need to know about finding a rental if you own one.

Service Animals vs. ESAs

Service animals and ESAs are two completely different categories, but they're often mixed up or treated as the same kind of pet.

On the one hand, service animals are trained to do specific tasks for people who cannot do those tasks themselves. For example, service animals might open doors, lead people who are unable to see, or alert deaf people to sounds. They can do countless other things as well, depending on the animal and person in question. Different service animals help different people.

On the other hand, ESAs provide their owners with therapeutic benefits. They act as companion animals for people with a mental-health condition or disability, such as anxiety or depression. They aren't trained to help with specific tasks the way that service animals are. Instead, their presence calms and stabilizes their owner. If a condition causes someone to experience unpleasant symptoms, having an ESA around can help to alleviate them. The key is that there is no particular training required for an animal to be an ESA.

Let's talk a little more about the different types of training that both kinds of pets receive and how the law differentiates between them. Then, we can talk about how all of this will impact your housing search.

What Kinds of Training Do Service Animals and ESAs Receive?

Service animals and ESAs have very different requirements when it comes to training. Service animals undergo an extensive training process specific to the needs of their owners. This training process can take anywhere from six months to a few years, depending on the type of service the animal will provide. Service-animal training can be conducted by a program or by the owner of the animal. These animals learn the tasks they are expected to perform under a variety of conditions created to reflect the real world. They practice their skills in different scenarios to ensure that they can perform a given task no matter how stressful or uncomfortable the surrounding environment is. Although it is not a legal requirement, service animals often wear harnesses or collars that indicate they are working animals.

ESAs do not require any training. In most cases, all that a person must have to indicate that their animal is an ESA is a letter from a health professional designating them as one.

How Does Housing Law Treat Service Animals and ESAs?

Generally speaking, the law treats service animals and ESAs differently. The Americans with Disabilities Act (ADA) ensures that people who have service animals can take them into almost any public space.

The same does not apply to ESAs. ESAs have limited legal rights and do not have access to all public spaces.

Housing law, however, treats the two types of animals the same. The US Department of Housing and Urban Development terms both service animals and ESAs as "assistance animals." A landlord may require a tenant to provide documentation for a service animal or an ESA. Most often, this is a doctor's note stating that the assistance animal in question alleviates the symptoms of the owner's disability.

From there on out, landlords deal with requests on a case-by-case basis. However, it is worth noting that the Fair Housing Act considers both service animals and ESAs a "reasonable accommodation." This means that landlords are only allowed to deny such requests under very specific conditions. These conditions include property damage, a threat to physical health or safety, a financial burden on the landlord, or an essential altering of the housing itself.

What Does Your Landlord Think When They Hear About Your ESA?

In the category of "you can't please all of the people all of the time" . . . many won't like this, but the first thing that is likely going to go through your landlord's mind when they hear about your ESA is that you're going to be a challenging renter.

In recent years, there has been a large number of self-reported ESAs. In some of these cases, people have used the ESA designation (legitimate or otherwise) as a way to get around apartment community rules that don't allow pets or specific breeds or to avoid pet rent and pet fees (that other residents are paying) that the landlord counts on to pay for costs and services related to pets in the community.

As a result, ESAs and their people have developed a bad reputation among landlords and other residents.

Is this bias deserved or undeserved? We'll let you be the judge of that. But we did promise to be honest with you, and we won't pull punches. If you have an ESA, it may make it more challenging for you to find a rental because of this bias.

Remember: It's more difficult to rent with a pet, but it's not impossible, especially if you understand exactly why landlords are wary of pets.

3.2

HOW TO DECIDE WHETHER A ROOMMATE IS RIGHT FOR YOU

Roommates can be super fun and helpful to have around, but as with all rental decisions, there are pros and cons. We're here to help you with everything, including understanding those pros and cons, actually finding a roommate, and living with a roommate successfully. Let's jump in.

WHY SHOULD YOU RENT WITH A ROOMMATE?

There are plenty of great reasons to have a roommate—or more than one, if you'd like. Here are some of the standout arguments in favor of a roommate:

- **You can split the rent.** It's nice to be able to split the rent with someone. Either you can save a bunch by splitting the cost of a place you were already planning to rent, or you can make your rental budget bigger after factoring in your roommate's financial contribution. You don't necessarily have to split the rent evenly; that all depends on what makes sense for you. We'll talk more about that later.
- **You'll have a built-in buddy.** Yay, friends! Your roommate can be someone to socialize with, if that's something you're interested in. It can be nice to come home to someone who wants to know about your day or who's up for drinks after work. You might pick a friend as your roommate, or you might become friends with your roommate after they move in. No matter how things go, it's likely that having a buddy built into your rental will come in handy sometimes.
- **You can be responsible for fewer chores.** Less rent, less chores—this roommate thing is sounding better and better, right? If you split chores, both of you can talk over exactly which chores you like and find ways to do the ones you prefer. Alternatively, you could rotate chores by having a chore chart. Either way, both of you are going to end up with a lot less work. That's good news because cleaning a whole apartment by yourself can take a lot of time and energy.
- **You'll have twice the decorating power.** Between your contributions and your roommate's, it will be easier to furnish and decorate an apartment. Things can look a little sparse if you don't have enough possessions to fill an entire living space, and that's the case for a lot of people. Plus, if you and your roommate move in at the same time, you can help each other move heavy stuff around and set things up the way you want them.

WHAT ARE SOME CONCERNS ABOUT RENTING WITH ROOMMATES?

We've talked about all of the best parts of having a roommate, but there can be conflicts, too. Let's go over a few cons to keep in mind when you're considering getting a roomie:

- **Working out the budget.** Splitting the budget is a win all around, but it can be tough to decide exactly how to split it. You could each take half, but that might not make sense for some roommate pairings. For example, maybe one of you makes a lot more money than the other does, or maybe one of you has a much bigger room than the other. You'll have to think carefully and be open and honest with each other to reach a solution that's smart and sustainable for both of you.
- **Sharing space.** You and your roommate will need to be on the same page about how much space you'll need, keeping your budget in mind. Will you have separate bedrooms? If one bedroom is much bigger than the other, who will take which bedroom? And will the person with the larger room pay more rent? How big of a living room and kitchen do you want? What style of apartment will you rent? All of your options will depend on your budget and the area you're living in, so you should make sure that the two of you are aligned in those priorities.
- **Dealing with noise.** Noise is one of the most common complaints between roommates. Shared living is always going to involve some amount of noise, so you should both be ready to make some compromises. However, when things start to get a little too loud, you and your roommate should be able to communicate with each other and work things out. Sometimes, it can help people to have certain rules, like instituting quiet hours at night. Whatever keeps the peace!
- **Handling messiness.** It's always unpleasant to have to clean up someone else's mess. Keeping your apartment clean is another common reason that roommates fight. Your roommate might

be comfortable with some dishes in the sink, while seeing dirty dishes lying around might make you very uncomfortable. It's definitely a good idea to make sure that you're on the same page about how clean you like things before you move in together.

- **Syncing schedules or not.** Whether or not your roommate's schedule will bother you depends on how much you want them to be a part of your life. If you want a social roommate who will spend time with you, it's wise to pick someone who has the same schedule as you so that you'll see each other at home. If you'd rather not interact with your roommate much, you can pick someone whose schedule is completely different from yours—you'll barely know you have a roommate.

HOW TO FIND A ROOMMATE

So, once you've thought through the pros and cons and decided you want a roommate, how do you go about finding one? We know it can be hard to find someone you're okay living with on a day-to-day basis. Here are a few of the most common methods for finding a roommate, along with each strategy's pros and cons.

- **Friends and family.** Renting with a friend or family member is a tried-and-true roommate method. The upsides are obvious: you know these people and you're pretty sure they aren't serial killers. You can trust them, and you enjoy spending time with them. These are strong pros when it comes to a roommate. There's one big con, though: if things go sour between you and your roommate, you might end up ruining your relationship with them. It's worth thinking about that possibility ahead of time.
- **Facebook groups.** Lots of neighborhoods have a Facebook group where people can look for roommates. Some cities even have Facebook groups for people who share certain traits, like being LGBTQIA+ or being from the same marginalized race. If these

are qualities that are important to you in a roommate, you can join these groups and see if anyone is your roommate match.

- **Websites and apps.** There is a plethora of different websites out there you can use to try to find a roommate. Some, like Roommates.com and Roomi, ask that you pay a subscription fee to talk with potential roommates. (It's annoying, of course, but paying also lowers the chances of being scammed.) Apps like RoomEasy offer a gamified, Tinder-esque setup. Take a look around at different websites and ask your friends for suggestions. You might find something that works for you.

THINGS TO KEEP IN MIND WHEN LOOKING FOR A ROOMMATE

We've talked about a few of the things that can screw up a roommate relationship: schedules, messiness, noise, and more. Those are all things you should talk about with any potential roommate. Here are a few other things you might want to think about as you meet and interview people you might room with:

- **Make sure the rental aligns with your needs.** Picking the right style of home or apartment can prove essential to your relationship with your roommate. Is there enough space in the kitchen for two people to move around each other, or will you have to take turns using the space? Are your bedrooms far enough apart to prevent or limit noise travel, or would a roommate wake you up if they moved around too much at night because your bedrooms share a wall?
- **Pick someone with whom you can communicate.** Communication is so essential to a good roommate relationship. Inevitably, problems will crop up, even if they're as small as someone leaving their dirty socks on the floor. You want your roommate to be someone you know you can talk to about any issue you're having with the state of the rental. Your roommate

should feel this way about you, too. It's always better to nip problems in the bud than to let anxiety and discomfort fester into resentment. You want to live with someone you can talk to.

- **Make sure your roommate can hold up their end of the bargain financially.** The last thing you want is to be worried about whether your roommate will be good for their share of the rent from one month to the next. We know that talking about money can be hard and awkward, but it's important to have conversations about whether your roommate is in a stable enough position to afford rent, utilities, and other housing costs. Besides, if they don't pay, usually you'll have to. And double rent is a heck of a burden to bear.

WRITING A ROOMMATE AGREEMENT

We've talked about a few different ways you can avoid or limit conflict between yourself and your roommate, like communicating clearly or maybe making a chore chart. Our top tip in this area, however, is to write a roommate agreement.

We'll explain what roommate agreements are, the different types of roommate agreements, and what a roommate agreement should include if you decide to write one.

What Is a Roommate Agreement?

A roommate agreement is a document that outlines the rules of your rental and the responsibilities of the tenants. You and your roommate would have a discussion about what life in your rental will look like and then write the agreement together before you move in. When you're happy with the agreement and you all agree on the rules you've laid out, you might all sign it, too. Importantly, a roommate agreement doesn't involve your landlord or property manager. It's only between the rental's tenants.

Hopefully, by having your ground rules in written form, you'll be able to refer to them during future conflicts. There'll be fewer misunderstandings between you and your roommate because the agreement will state what the rules are.

What Should Be Included in a Roommate Agreement?

You can put any kinds of rules you want in a roommate agreement. However, there are a few major points we'd suggest hitting:

- **Rent.** Who's paying what portion of the rent? Are you splitting it evenly? Dividing it up proportionate to your incomes? Is the person with the bigger room paying a larger share? Whatever the case may be, you'll want to have it written down.
- **Security deposit.** Yep, this, too. Who's paying what part of it? What happens to the security deposit if one person moves out and the other stays? What happens to the returned security deposit if you both move out at the same time?
- **Utilities.** As with the rent, you'll want to put down in writing how you'll share responsibility for utilities. Will you take turns paying the utilities each month? What about dividing the utilities up by who is using them? Will you split them evenly?
- **Division of space.** Who will get each room in the rental? If there's an office, who gets it, or will you share it? How will closets or the refrigerator be divided?
- **Chores.** Chores can be a sore spot, as we've discussed, so getting your rules down in writing is a good idea. Write down how you'll divvy up your chores and what you'll do if someone doesn't do their share. Keep in mind each other's schedules and who uses which appliances or spaces the most. You can also consider creating a chore chart.
- **Pets.** If some or one of you own pets, you should write down your plan for keeping them clean and fed. You might also want to consider the following questions: What rooms of the rental will the pet be allowed in? Is the pet allowed on the furniture? How often will it be groomed? Who will be responsible for cleaning the pet's messes and feeding it? Who will pay for damages caused by the pet? What happens if the neighbors

complain about the pet? Write down all of the pertinent information in the agreement to avoid conflict later.

- **Guests.** You and your roommate will need to discuss what your rules will be around hosting guests in your rental. Will overnight guests be allowed? How often? Does this have to be discussed beforehand when it happens? What if someone wants to throw a party? How many people can be invited?
- **Noise level.** Noise can be another sore spot. When, if ever, will loud music be allowed in the apartment? Will you decide to have quiet hours? If so, when will they be? What if someone won't stop being loud—how will you handle it? These questions are particularly important if anyone in your rental works from home.
- **Moving out early.** What will you do if someone wants to move out early? Will they have to sublet to someone else (if allowed by the landlord)? Will they just pay the remainder of their rent for the rest of the lease? Think through what that might look like and come to a solution you and your roommate both feel comfortable with. After all, even if no one is planning to move out early, you never know when an issue or an emergency might arise.

Besides these suggestions, you should put anything that's important to you or your roommate into your roommate agreement. The more information you have, the lower the chances of a problem arising later.

ADDING A ROOMMATE AFTER YOU SIGN YOUR LEASE

What if you decide you want a roommate later, after you've signed your lease? You'll have to talk about it with your landlord and get their approval before the new roommate moves in. If your landlord says yes, they'll have to write up a new lease because your roommate will also have to sign it.

Your landlord might decide to raise your rent or your security deposit if you add a roommate. More people living in the apartment means more "wear and tear," which means more repair costs—hence the potential rent increase. As for the security-deposit increase, more people also means more potential for serious damage, and your landlord will want to be ready for that possibility as well. (Check your local laws to see if there's a maximum-allowed security deposit, and if there is, make sure that your landlord doesn't ask for more than that amount.) If your landlord decides to raise any of these costs, you can decide with your new roommate whether it still makes financial sense to move in together. You can always negotiate with your landlord—head back to Section 2.10 for more on that.

Remember: **Writing a roommate agreement can prevent conflict, so go the extra mile and put your ground rules on paper.**

3.3

HOW TO FIND A PLACE WHEN YOU HAVE BAD CREDIT OR NO CREDIT

As we've mentioned, having a bad credit score—or no credit score at all—is a common problem, especially for newer renters. This section is dedicated to helping you overcome this obstacle on your rental application because a credit score is something the vast majority of landlords will want to know.

WHY DO LANDLORDS CARE ABOUT CREDIT?

If you're frustrated about your credit score, you might be wondering why credit matters so much in the first place. Your credit score is supposed to be a reflection of how much debt you have and how well and promptly you've paid it back over time. Because a landlord will be collecting rent from you, they'll want to know that you're good at making payments on time. They might consider a credit score one measure of how reliably you might make rent payments.

We know that you might not feel that your credit score is an accurate reflection of how good you are at paying back your debt. If you're saddled with a big amount of debt, like a student loan, your score may be lower than you'd like, even if you've never missed a payment. In addition to improving your credit or establishing credit for the first time, you've got a few different ways you can show a potential landlord that you'll pay rent reliably.

DISCUSS YOUR PROBLEM WITH YOUR LANDLORD

We know, we know: we're singing the same old tune again. But we're serious! If you're worried about your credit score during your rental application process, mention it to the landlord right up front. You can put it as a note into your application itself, or you can even organize a meeting or a phone call to discuss your circumstances.

Doing this shows your landlord that you already have a handle on your credit problem, which might give their confidence a boost. Additionally, it will show your landlord that you're honest and up-front about your problems—qualities of a great tenant.

MAKE SURE YOUR REFERENCES ARE STRONG

We've talked a little about references already. It's extra important to make sure that you have good references when your credit score is low. Your references should be people who can place emphasis on the fact that you're a timely and reliable person who wouldn't miss a payment. Former landlords are great if you've got them. Otherwise, employers or supervisors are good options.

THINGS YOU CAN OFFER TO OFFSET YOUR CREDIT

You can offer a potential landlord a few things as a tenant to offset any concerns they might have about your lower credit score. Your landlord will consider themself to be taking a financial risk if they take on a tenant with a lower credit score. In return, you want to offer something to lessen that risk. This could include:

- A roommate with good credit
- A larger security deposit
- A longer lease
- And, last but not least . . .

YOU COULD GET SOMEONE TO COSIGN YOUR LEASE

If your landlord is really worried about your credit score, you could offer to have someone cosign your lease, or they may issue you a "conditional approval" that requires you to have a cosigner.

A cosigner (also called a "guarantor") is someone who doesn't live in the apartment with you but whose name is still on your lease. Your cosigner will be held responsible if you can't or won't fulfill the terms of your lease. Think about a cosigner as a form of insurance for a landlord. If you fall through somehow, your cosigner will pick up the slack.

Oftentimes, a landlord won't tell you that you need a cosigner until after your rental application has been processed. If you know your credit score is low, though, you can get a jump on the situation and start thinking about who to ask to be your cosigner.

Who Should You Ask?

First, a cosigner should be an adult you trust. This could be a relative or a friend—whoever makes most sense for you. Your cosigner should understand your financial situation and trust you to uphold your part of the lease.

Remember, this person will be responsible if you can't make rent or if you damage your rental. You want to be sure to pick someone who is not only able but also willing to do that. They should be able to handle any financial repercussions, including the possibility that their credit score could take a dip.

A cosigner will likely need to have an income equivalent to four or five times the apartment's rent, at minimum.

In addition to individuals who can act as a cosigner, there are now several companies that offer cosigning as a service. Usually, the way it works is they will provide a guarantee to your landlord, which usually clears the way for you to live in the place even with bad credit—but unlike your family or friend cosigner, these companies will charge you a fee for the service.

This is a developing service offering, and we expect more companies to offer this service over time. Check out the Dwellsy blog for an ever-growing list of cosigning firms: Dwellsy.com/blog/co-signers.

A Cosigner's Responsibilities

A cosigner goes through the same application process as the rest of the tenants and has to be approved by the landlord. Usually, there is no criminal check run on cosigners because they will not live in the rental. After being approved, the cosigner becomes liable for any payments the tenants miss, deposits they cannot make, or damages they cause. The cosigner holds these responsibilities with regard to every tenant on the lease, regardless of which tenants they may know personally. Keep that in mind if/when you choose to rent with roommates.

Potential Problems

Obviously, there's always a chance that the person you choose as your cosigner could end up on the hook for your missed rent or damages. You don't want to ruin your relationship with your cosigner or put them in a bad financial spot. It's a good idea to have a serious talk with your cosigner to make sure you both understand the risks and that you have a plan in place if things go wrong. Your cosigner could be the key to you landing the perfect rental, and hopefully they'll be pleased to help.

Remember: Being straightforward about your bad credit is your best bet, so make sure you talk to a potential landlord about your credit score once you've applied.

3.4

HOW TO FIND THE ELUSIVE SINGLE-FAMILY RENTAL HOME

Single-family homes are tough to rent. No two ways about it.

They make up about one out of every three rentals in the United States, so you'd think they'd be easier to find, but because they're widely spread out and there's lots of demand for them, that's just not the case.

So how do you go about finding one if that's what you want?

PRO TIP 1: KNOW WHERE TO LOOK

The first key is to know where to look for single-family rentals. Unfortunately, the legacy pay-to-play listing platforms are built to serve the owners and operators of large apartment complexes, so you won't find much in the way of single-family rentals there.

Happily, Dwellsy does have a ton of single-family rentals, and there are other platforms that have some single-family rentals as well, including Rent.com and Zillow.

After you've checked online listings, walking or driving through your desired neighborhood is the next-best strategy. Again, this can be challenging because any for-rent signs you see may have been up for a little while already, so it can be hard to know which listings are freshly available. But other than checking Dwellsy, this is usually the most productive thing you can do to find single-family rental options.

PRO TIP 2: KNOW WHAT YOU WANT

More so than with any other type of rental, those of us who are looking for single-family homes are doing so for a specific reason.

Maybe you need to be in a certain school district, maybe you need proximity to work or family, maybe you need a certain amount of backyard space for your dog, or maybe you need a particular setup to accommodate working from home.

Whatever your personal situation is, make sure you are very clear on what you need to have so that you can quickly evaluate what works for you and what doesn't.

If you want more guidance about how to think through this, check out Section 2.2 for the Dwellsy approach to prioritization.

PRO TIP 3: BE FIRST

More so than with any other type of rental, to get the single-family home that you want, you need to move fast.

These types of rentals typically get a lot of interest very quickly; it's not uncommon for a new single-family home listing to get fifty inquiries in the first day.

And you'll remember from Section 2.5 the importance of not just being fast but being first. As a quick reminder, the first inquiry for a rental has about a 50 percent chance of getting the place, and the fifth inquiry has less than a 5 percent chance of getting the place.

Because landlords for single-family rentals can get so many inquiries on the first day, it's more important to be first for these properties than for any other type of rental.

Also recall that if you're genuinely interested in a place, we consider it best practice to submit both an email and a phone inquiry because different landlords have different beliefs about which one they respond to first. Submitting both an email and a phone inquiry gives you two shots at being first and protects you in case the landlord is looking at one type of inquiry and not the other.

PRO TIP 4: BE FAST

If you don't move quickly, someone else will, and they'll get the place. Don't let that happen to you.

You've done the right thing by focusing on being the first inquiry and submitting both email and phone inquiries.

Now, be sure to make everything else happen quickly when you hear from the landlord.

First, book the first available showing. Don't limit the showing only to when it's most convenient for you—you need to take the first showing that the landlord will book and adjust your schedule to make it work.

Second, be ready to complete the application and put down a deposit on the place when you see it if the rental looks good to you. These places go fast, and if you're the first to see it, protect your advantage by moving to the next step quickly.

That means filling out an application and putting a holding deposit down there on the spot. So, bring to the showing your form of payment and everything that you expect to need for the application. If possible, bring a tablet or laptop in case you need to submit the application electronically so you can complete it while you're there.

Third, when your application is approved (assuming it is), make sure you get the lease quickly and that you sign the lease. And be ready to pay the up-front costs of the rental, whether first and last month's rent, a security deposit, or other fees.

Remember: Single-family homes are hard to find—there's no doubt about that. By using the same skills we've talked about for apartments, like being fast and first in line, you'll give yourself the best possible shot at getting one.

3.5

HOW TO FIND A PLACE FAST

One of the more challenging searches that we hear about here at Dwellsy is the rental hunt that has to be done as soon as possible.

There are any number of reasons why this might be the case. Maybe you just landed a job in a new city and they want you to start right away. Maybe your current place is no longer right for you and you need to move out right away. Maybe you've just run out of time on your search.

Whatever the reason, there are some shortcuts that can help you find a place quickly. And we're talking about a "within a couple of days" kind of fast.

The most important thing is to establish what you absolutely need and separate those things from the nice-to-have items. The following are some of the items that tend to rise to the top of the pile in this situation:

- **Budget.** This is often highly inflexible, so know how much room you have to move on price and how important this is to you.
- **Proximity to a job, family, childcare, or friends, or other location-based factors.** Location can be a critical driver in how well a

place works for you. If you have to drive ninety minutes to get to and from work, that can really create issues.

- **Pet requirements.** Pets are among the most challenging. For those of us who are pet owners, it's simply not negotiable to leave Fido or Fluffy behind.

Whatever your unique situation is, you know best what's most important to you. What's critical is to be honest with yourself about what you can and cannot trade off so that you can move quickly.

Once you have identified what you absolutely need, then you can use a few strategies to target the types of places that tend to have availability.

Speedy Strategy 1: Search Big Apartment Communities

Whether a fifty-story tower or a rambling three-hundred-apartment garden-style community, large apartment communities almost always have some availability and can usually accommodate the need to move in quickly.

When you're looking at Dwellsy listings, look for the kinds of places that have numerous open units at a single location.

These places are not without their trade-offs, but they can be a great option for many folks, and, as we all know, sometimes the best option is the one that's available.

These big communities are generally well-equipped with things like easy parking, package receiving, and amenities like pools and gyms. Plus, they tend to be very well maintained. Often, these properties are really easy to work with, as they offer professional management, on-site maintenance staff, and the ability to pay your rent and submit maintenance requests online or through an app.

Some folks love the clean, standardized nature of these properties, and others find them too cookie-cutter or sterile, but we'll leave that up to your individual taste.

The biggest downside of these properties is that they tend to be full priced. One of the reasons why they generally have some availability is that they're able to get top market rent and are usually willing to leave some units open for a little longer to make sure they're getting the most rent they can.

Speedy Strategy 2: Use Apartment Locators/Brokers

In many parts of the country (but not all), there are local apartment locators. These are folks who will accompany you in the rental search for a fee—usually a full month's rent, more or less.

New York City is famous (notorious?) for its locators and brokers. It's actually one of those rare places where it's nearly impossible to find a place on your own and you're virtually forced to work with a broker since that's how leasing is done in that market.

In many other big cities, particularly those in the Northeast, brokers/locators are an option but not a necessity for a more typical search. They can, however, be incredibly valuable when you need to move quickly.

The locator works with you by understanding your preferences and then touring you around properties they have in their inventory. In many cases, they will actually drive you around, and often you will see enough good options in the course of a few hours or a single day that you can pick the best of them with confidence.

There are two major catches with locators. First, there's a significant cost involved. In most markets, it's paid by the landlord, but in New York City, you have to pay the locator directly. Again, it's usually about a month's rent. If you're paying the fee, the cost is obvious, but if the landlord is paying the fee, it's less apparent—but you should know that their cost is then built into the rent, so you'd still be paying it, even though it may not feel like it.

The second major catch is that their inventory tends to be quite limited. Locators only work with landlords who are willing to pay them to bring renters, and most landlords are not willing to pay their fees and instead do their own leasing.

But, if you're in a hurry, locators can get the job of finding a place done quickly.

Speedy Strategy 3: Do It Yourself

The classic search for a place can be done by yourself, but the key is to move quickly at every stage and to be ready to lease on the spot.

In theory, an actual search shouldn't take that long, but it typically takes several weeks or longer, mostly because every renter is looking for the best place for them and would prefer not to accept trade-offs.

The three keys to doing it yourself are:

1. **Block time for the search.** Doing a rental search during a few minutes carved out here and there during your workday is not going to cut it. Find a way to set aside an entire day or two for the search, and make sure you have access to transportation to get around to different places.
2. **Decide quickly.** Be ready to put down a deposit and maybe even sign a lease on the spot while you're touring. Hopefully, you've been able to see a handful of places, so when you get to one that's better for you than the others are, go for it.
3. **Accept trade-offs.** Maybe you wanted a dishwasher or washing machine in your unit, but since you need to move quickly, you might not get those or other things that are important but optional.

Remember: You're going to have to make some tough choices if you want something fast, so it's important to stay cool and rational.

3.6

HOW TO FIND A PLACE WHEN YOU DON'T LIVE THERE

The remote search is one of the biggest challenges a searching renter can face. Finding a place is tough enough when you're in town, but to have to do so when you can't be there in person is just so much harder.

So, how to attack this particularly challenging search? Here are all the pro tips you need to get this tough search done.

PRO TIP 1: KNOW YOUR TIMING, KNOW YOUR NEEDS

Most of us are pretty responsive to what we discover when we search. You may go out looking for something specific but then throw everything you had in mind out the window when you walk into a place that unexpectedly feels like home.

That approach is great when you're in town and can stand in the house or apartment and know that it's the one. When you're out of town, though, you won't get that firsthand experience, so you'll need to set yourself up for success by being pretty honest with yourself about what you can and can't live without to make sure the place you find checks all the boxes you need it to.

Check out Section 2.2 for all the details on prioritization, including the Dwellsy approach to getting organized.

PRO TIP 2: PRIORITIZE YOUR SAFETY

Unfortunately for you, remote searchers are by far the most susceptible to fraudster strategies. Because you're not there in person, you can't do the most important thing to stay safe—see the place in person. That makes it much harder to have the context helpful for deciding whether a place makes sense within the area around it or whether it's too good to be true.

All is not lost, however. You can stay safe. Check out our section on rental fraud and how to keep yourself safe (Section 1.5) for all the details, but here are a few of the most critical points to remember for a remote search:

- Keep the search clean from the beginning by only using trusted sites like Dwellsy to make sure you're looking at legitimate places—and stay far, far away from the most fraud-riddled sites, like Craigslist.
- Make sure you're dealing with real people as your landlords. Real people have an internet presence and are willing to do a video or voice call with you.
- Even if you can't get inside the place, if you're talking to a real landlord, they can get inside the place, so use that to your advantage. Ask them to do a live video tour via FaceTime, Zoom, or Google Meet.
- Don't spend any time trying to figure out if something is too good to be true. If the price is lower than you'd expect or the place seems too good to be true in any way, just leave it. It's not worth the risk, and it's too difficult to figure out if it's legit from far away.

- Be wary and walk away at the first sign of anything weird. Landlord wants money up front before signing the lease? Walk away. Landlord wants a big "showing deposit"? Walk away. Landlord won't talk on video? Walk away.

Again, this is the riskiest kind of rental search you can do, so please take a look at Section 1.5 for all the details on how to stay safe.

PRO TIP 3: FIND A FRIEND

If you can't be in person to tour an apartment, it's great to find someone who can. In most cases, when you're moving to a new place, it's because you know someone there. And they're likely excited that you, their friend, is moving to their area!

Channel that emotional support and excitement about your arrival to get help from these folks because they can be a huge asset to you on the ground in your search. They can tour places when you can't, they can drive through the neighborhood and tell you what they think, they can look the property manager in the eye and ask the in-person questions that are on your mind, and they can turn on the shower and find out if the water pressure is awesome or pathetic. Don't hesitate to ask for help!

PRO TIP 4: CONSIDER GOING PRO

Professional property managers aren't necessarily better or worse than independent landlords once you've moved into a place, but they are usually more organized through the leasing process, which makes you better able to rent when you're not present in person.

These managers have a professional set of processes and systems that makes it much easier to run through the leasing process remotely, and if you're considering a place that has an on-site property-management office, it's very easy for them to do helpful things like give you a video tour of the unit.

Plus, it is usually much easier to evaluate the safety of these landlords. They should all have a website and professional email addresses, and almost all will be using professional software to manage the leasing process. These are all signs that the listing is legitimate and that you're going through a safe process.

PRO TIP 5: PLAN A VISIT

While many are not able to do this, you can in theory pack a lot of rental hunting into a weekend or even a single day. If you can get to your new town for a day or two of searching, it can be a huge help.

Start by doing your online research, and get as specific about what you're looking for as possible. The most important factors are neighborhood, price point, and any deal killers. If you have a big dog, know that you're not going to have time to convince anyone that he's as lovable as you know he is. You'll need to know up front that they'll take him without question.

Next, when you're within a couple of days of your visit, start lining up appointments and booking specific times and locations of rentals you want to see. It's helpful to map the visits so you know how much time it will take to get from place to place and can ensure that you have time for all your visits. Jonas once saw eleven places in a particularly grueling one-day search. If you don't hear back from a landlord, just move on to the next. Unfortunately, with this kind of visit, there's no time to waste; they need to fit into your schedule, not the other way around.

If you're open to working with a professional management company, this process can get much easier because it'll generally have a range of places available, and you can choose from what they have, even if the place you were excited about online has already been rented.

Another great option for this short visit is to work with a locator if they're available in the area you're moving to. Reach out to them in advance to tell them what you're looking for and line up an appointment to work with one of their team members for the day or days you'll be there. Check out Section 3.5 for more information about locator services.

Remember: Whether you ask a landlord or a friend, asking for help is important to a virtual search. Don't be afraid to ask for more pictures or for someone to scope out a place for you.

3.7

HOW TO GET AND USE SECTION 8 AND OTHER HOUSING VOUCHERS

The good news for renters struggling to afford rent is that there's a variety of rental-assistance resources available (often called just "Section 8") that can help. Over ten million Americans get some measure of financial help through these vouchers or related programs from the federal government.[6]

The bad news is that many of these various programs are a mess. They're incredibly complicated, and in most places, there are long waiting lists to get rental assistance.

And when we say long, we mean *really* long—more than a decade, in some cases. In 2022, a Chicago woman finally received a housing voucher after a twenty-nine-year wait.[7] Needless to say, she'd moved on and found other options nearly thirty years earlier.

GETTING RENTAL ASSISTANCE

These programs are administered by a patchwork quilt of programs across the country. In some cases, they're city-specific, and in others, they're statewide. Some are private, and some are funded by governmental entities.

The federal Department of Housing and Urban Development (HUD) maintains a list of all of the contacts for the various HUD programs for rental assistance on its website.

We wish we could provide you with more information about how to go through this process. Unfortunately, each entity has a unique approach to running its program, and it's best to contact each one directly to find out how it approaches things. Of course, you'll want to understand the expected wait time and if it's even worth your time to go through the process. With wait times of twenty-nine years in some places, it likely doesn't even make sense for many to go through the process, unfortunately.

A Section 8 voucher, or a housing-choice voucher, is a form of rental assistance from public housing agencies. Vouchers allow low-income families, elderly people, and disabled people to choose their own housing in the private market while the government subsidizes part of the rent. Once the person or family with the voucher finds housing, and if the landlord agrees to take the voucher, a public housing agency will cover most of the rent, and the renter makes up the difference.

USING A VOUCHER

If you're one of the lucky ones with a Section 8 voucher or a promise of other rental assistance, congrats! Now, how do you use it?

In some parts of the country (but not all), landlords are required to accept Section 8 vouchers or other rental-assistance payments. In many cases, it makes good business sense for landlords to rent to someone with a guarantee of at least partial rent payment from a third party, so the landlord may be willing to accept rental-assistance payments even if not legally required to.

Renters with rental assistance do tend to be very long-term tenants, and the government is a very dependable payer, so landlords who have Section 8 or other assisted tenants in their properties generally report lower expenses due to turnover and vacancy than do other landlords. Hence why it makes good business sense to accept third-party rental assistance.

So, acceptance shouldn't be a problem. Why are we saying "shouldn't"? Because those with rental assistance do often have trouble finding a landlord willing to accept their vouchers.

Why? Have we mentioned how important it is to be able to move quickly in the rental-search process? Maybe once or twice, right?

Well, unfortunately, there's nothing fast about vouchers. Using a Section 8 voucher requires a cooperative landlord who's willing to comply with the government rules and regulations necessary to accept the voucher, and they need to be willing to wait for government approvals that, at best, take several weeks and, at worst, can take a month or more.

If you're a landlord looking to get a place rented, you usually have just thirty days from when you first find out that you'll have a vacancy until you might actually have a vacant place.

Landlords in this period of time want to move quickly, and waiting on government bureaucracy to approve paperwork is the kind of thing that sounds like it will lead to vacancy.

So, in most cases, landlords run their normal process with rentals, responding to the first inquiries and accepting the first renter who is approved and pays the rent. Typically, that whole process takes a couple of days, leaving no time for a voucher-use approval process. That's how rental-assistance users lose out.

So, if you're one of those folks using some form of rental assistance, you need to use your understanding of how the process works to your advantage and think like a landlord.

Here are three tips to make it more likely for you to find a place that will accept your voucher.

Voucher-Use Tip 1: Live in a Big Community

Big communities tend to always have a handful of available units, so you can apply for several apartments, or, in some cases, just get approved for "any apartment" in that community, and then move forward with one that becomes available.

A sub-tip to this tip is that a big community is somewhat more likely to have a local ordinance that prohibits "source of income" discrimination in housing. If "source of income" is a protected class under local or state law (it's not protected under the federal Fair Housing Act), a landlord can't refuse to rent to someone just based on the source of the applicant's lawful income, even if that "income" includes rental-assistance payments.

Voucher-Use Tip 2: Look for a Big Property-Management Company

Because big property-management companies manage big portfolios, they almost always have some availability in their system. Find the biggest property-management companies in your area and get to know one of their leasing reps.

The leasing rep may or may not understand how rental assistance works, so you should expect to have to educate them on the process. But once they know that you need a little extra time for the approval process and understand a little about what they'll need to do, they should be able to help you. Remember, they're busy, and they may not remember to reach out to you when they have a place available, but you can watch their portfolio on their website or on a site like Dwellsy. When you see a place that's available, it's time to call that leasing agent.

Voucher-Use Tip 3: Look for a Property Manager with a Mission

In most larger cities and many smaller ones, there are property managers who have a mission to serve the underserved. These managers often specialize in moderate-cost rentals ("affordable housing") and are very comfortable with the various processes around the use of rental assistance, especially Section 8 vouchers.

> **Remember:** Casting a wide net is helpful here: look at several large apartment communities, get to know several leasing agents, and apply for several apartments at a time.

3.8

HOW TO FIND OFF-CAMPUS HOUSING AS A COLLEGE STUDENT

If you're renting as a college student, this section is for you.

Some colleges and universities offer their own on-campus dormitories, and dorm living is a great option for some students. However, many students choose to live in off-campus housing. Living off campus will be the first time many students encounter the rental process. Let's talk about what resources you have available as a student renter and how your rental experience might differ from the norm.

PROS AND CONS OF LIVING OFF CAMPUS

In case you haven't decided whether to live on or off campus yet, it might help to go over the basic pros and cons of living off campus. Obviously, these will differ depending on the school and the surrounding area, but we've collected a few of the most common ones.

The pros:

- **Cheaper housing.** Off-campus housing is usually cheaper than paying for a dorm. Dorms often include meal plans and other amenities, including the convenience of living on campus, so you pay a premium. Getting your own rental can save you quite a bit.
- **More space.** Dorm rooms are often quite tiny, with room for only a bed, a desk, and a closet, so there's an excellent chance you'll end up with a bigger place if you live off campus, whether that's in an apartment or a house.
- **A full kitchen.** There's no way around it: dining-hall food can suck. It can be expensive, too. Having access to a kitchen and the ability to buy your own groceries and cook your own meals instead can be a blessing, especially if you're a competent cook.
- **Fewer rules.** In a dorm, there will likely be tons of rules, from the types of appliances you can keep in your room to how many guests you can have over at a time. If you rent off campus, there will certainly be some rules in your lease, but they won't be nearly as strict.
- **Decorating freedom.** Some dorms are quite restrictive in terms of what you can put on your walls. There are a few that have total bans on things like posters and fairy lights. You'll run into fewer restrictions of this type if you live off campus in an apartment or house.
- **No school-housing lotteries.** Lots of schools have random lotteries or similar ways of deciding who gets what room. Obviously, there's always a chance you won't come out on top, and you might not feel like trying your luck. That's particularly true if you're a first-year student and there's some sort of ranking based on seniority. If you rent a place off campus, you won't have to worry about any of that; you can take more control over choosing the place where you'll live.

On the other hand, a few of the cons:

- **Fewer amenities.** Dorms will often come packed with amenities that allow you to focus on studying, like having cleaning staff make regular rounds or having laundry facilities in your building. (These services are partly how they justify the more expensive price tag.) If you rent off campus, you're not guaranteed these things, so you might end up doing more cleaning, cooking, and other types of housekeeping.
- **Living far from campus.** One of the biggest benefits of living in a dorm is the proximity to campus. When you've got five minutes until class starts and you're still scrambling to get your laptop in your bag, it's important to be as close to the academic buildings as you can. If you live off campus, you might have a bit of a trek, or even a drive, to your classes. This is also a negative if your campus is the social hub of your school. You might find yourself attending fewer social events because you don't want to bother going all the way to campus. If you're a first-year student, living away from campus can be particularly isolating in that way.
- **More concerns about being evicted or unhoused.** School housing is likely to be more lenient in terms of lease breaking and rent payment. They'll probably be more sympathetic to your needs as a student and will work something out with you in the event of an emergency rather than evict you. A traditional landlord, however, will probably care less that you're a student and might evict you if you break the lease.

WHERE TO FIND OFF-CAMPUS HOUSING

If you decide to live off campus, you'll be far from the first student to look for housing in the area. Landlords around campus will be ready for the inevitable wave of students every fall. The school itself will probably have its own slew of resources to support you, especially if a large portion of its student body lives off campus.

This means that ways to find housing will probably make themselves known once you mention that you'll be living off campus. Other students will likely be full of suggestions as to where you should live, and some might even offer themselves as roommates.

Let's talk about the different ways you can find a rental.

Your School Can Still Help

Some schools have such a sizable population of students living off campus that they have their own rental boards. This is particularly true for larger schools—the University of Washington's Eau Claire campus and the University of Texas at Austin are two examples. The school will probably vet the landlords whom they allow to list on these housing boards, so one benefit of using them is that you're less likely to run into a scam. Sometimes, schools even make deals with certain landlords. Check to see if your school has any resources like these.

Student-Specific Rental Sites

There are several sites out there that are specifically for students looking for housing near their schools. Here are a few:

- **Dwellsy.** We have rentals of all kinds on Dwellsy, and that includes a great selection of student rentals. You can find these by searching the town you'd like to rent in, clicking on the "Filters" button, scrolling to "Lifestyle," and then listing "Student Housing" as either a "Want" or a "Need," depending on how high of a priority it is that you're in student-specific housing.
- **ForRentUniversity.** ForRentUniversity.com is a branch of ForRent.com that is specifically tailored to college and university students. If you search by school, the listings that come up show their distance from campus.
- **Student.com.** Student.com has an inventory of rentals around the world, including many American college towns. Its listings show what is included in your rent, the distance to campus, and a number of other useful things. It's important to highlight that

you can search by cancellation policy if you're still waiting on a visa or an acceptance letter.

- **University Living.** UniversityLiving.com is another rental site used by students all over the world. It has listings in major American cities but not in lots of other college towns. Its listings also include flexible cancellation plans, distance to campus, and amenities.

The Traditional Rental Market

Of course, you can try your hand at traditional rentals through Dwellsy and similar sites. The rest of this book can help you if that's what you want to do. Landlords in your town or city will likely expect applications from students anyway, especially if you attend a larger school. You might get beat out by a professional with a steadier income or a longer credit history, but who knows? Maybe your ideal rental situation is on the market right now.

WHAT KIND OF RENTAL DO YOU WANT?

You'll want to put some thought into what kind of rental you're looking for. Your choices might be limited to apartments or houses, but there might also be some dorm-style private housing around your school if the off-campus population is big enough, so you should look into the options that are specific to your area.

It might be tempting to rent a house and cram in with a bunch of roommates—a classic situation that has successfully housed many students. Consider, however, that houses usually come with tons more upkeep than apartments do. Since houses are bigger, you'll also have to spend more time cleaning them. That means you'll want to be sure your roommates will share the work equally and that the mess won't build up throughout your rental. Moreover, you'll have to share the kitchen and appliances with everyone else.

Apartments are smaller and usually easier to manage in terms of upkeep. If you're a social butterfly, though, you might have less room to host people, especially if you have a studio. These are the kinds of considerations that you want to keep in mind as a student.

Consider your study habits when you think about the style of your rental, too. If the place is furnished, does it come with a desk and chair? Those can be expensive, especially if you want them to be comfortable. Maybe that won't matter if you tend to study in the library or at a coffee shop, though. Or maybe you don't like to study in your room, and you'd prefer to do it in the kitchen or the common area of the apartment or house. Will it be quiet enough there? Will your roommates give you the space and privacy you need to study that way?

These are the kinds of questions you'll need to ask yourself concerning your priorities as a student. Of course, the answers will differ from person to person and from area to area. Figure out what you need, what you can afford, and what's available where you're looking.

THE LENGTH OF YOUR LEASE

The duration of your lease is another thing you should consider as you're looking for an off-campus rental. Lots of landlords who rent to students will offer a lease that spans the school year, which is perfect for many, since they'd like to stay with their parents or elsewhere over the summer. Maybe that's the case for you. But maybe you'd rather stay near campus and work a job in your school's town over the summer, so you want a lease that will cover the summer months.

You might not even know what your plan is that far ahead of time, though, and many students don't. Some landlords will offer flexible month-to-month leases, so you could go that route to avoid being locked into a particular living situation. It's up to you!

> **Remember:** You'll be in this boat with other students. Use student group chats and resources offered by your university for support and advice.

Section 4
MOVING IN AND MAKING THE MOST OF YOUR PLACE

Hooray, the hardest part is over! The search is over, the apartment is picked, and the lease is signed. Congratulations! We bet you can't wait to get settled into your new home.

Don't worry—we'll be around to help with this next step, too. In this section, we'll cover:

- Getting utilities set up
- Renters insurance, maintenance, emergencies, and other useful stuff
- Moving out of your old place and into your new one
- How to have good relationships with your roommates, landlord, and neighbors
- Sprucing up the place, furnishing it, and keeping it pest-free
- What to do if your landlord is selling your rental
- What to do if things go wrong

Sound good? Let's kick it off by talking about getting your utilities set up, which is usually the first thing you'll want to do once you've got your new place.

4.1

SETTING UP YOUR UTILITIES

Ah, power. And water. And gas, internet, sewer, trash, cable TV, and, and, and . . .

All, or at least most, of these utilities are essential, but how and when do you get them set up?

You don't want to be in your place on the first night unable to turn on the lights, so let's make sure you know what you need to do to get everything going.

For most rentals, you should find that many of the utility services are already in place, so the task you need to do is to get everything transferred to your name.

How does this transition work? Well, for utilities like power, water, gas, and sewer, it's difficult (and costly) for the utility companies to actually turn the service off between tenants because they would need to send someone out to your new place in order to turn it on or off.

Also, there are lots of systems that need to be running even if there's no one living there, or else trouble will ensue. For example, if the gas is turned off and the place is unheated in the winter, water pipes could freeze, and the place could get flooded—a disaster for the landlord and anyone else in the building.

So, rather than create the risk of that kind of disaster, what they do instead of turning the utility off is make an "accounting change" in which they just change who's responsible for payment.

When a renter moves out of a place and tells the utility companies they've moved out, the responsibility for payment transfers to the landlord, and when you move into your new place, the responsibility needs to transfer to you.

TRANSFERRING THE UTILITIES TO YOUR NAME

If you're moving in, the first thing is to find out which utilities you'll be responsible for according to your lease agreement and which companies provide those utilities in your area. This is different in every part of the country and sometimes varies even within the same metro area, so the best way to determine current utility providers is to find out from your landlord which utility company provides which services. Your landlord can also confirm what you're responsible for and what they're responsible for. For instance, you might be responsible for gas and electricity, and your landlord might pay for water and trash/recycling.

You should also find out if there's any specific information that the utilities will require to turn service on. Sometimes utilities have a unique identifier for the property, something like a parcel number or an account number, and your landlord should be able to provide you with that.

With that info in hand, in most cases, you can go to a utility company's website or call it to get service transferred into your name. Usually, this will require several calls—one for power, one for gas, one for water, etc. In some regions, there are utility companies that handle more than one utility, and, in rare cases, there are utility companies that handle everything, requiring you to make just one call.

Regardless, make sure you have the key utilities covered: power, water, gas, sewer, and trash/recycling.

When you get utilities turned on, it's critical that they're turned on by the date on which you move in, so it's often prudent to take responsibility a day or two before that date just to make sure there are no hiccups along the way and allow some space in the timeline if there are.

Usually, you want to set up your utilities accounts about two weeks before you move into your place. If you have less time, it's usually not a problem, especially if things are being transferred into your name and there's no new service to set up. There are different steps involved when setting up a new utility service.

SETTING UP A NEW UTILITY SERVICE

You might move into a brand-new or renovated place that is getting utility service set up for the first time, or you might end up in a place where it's more common to cut off service between residents. Most commonly, some sort of mistake has been made to result in service being turned off.

No matter the reason, the process is similar to when utilities just need to be transferred into your name, with two key differences.

First, there will be a site visit from the utilities company or companies. When service is already on, they can just change the responsible party, but in most cases when it's turned off, they need to send a utility employee out to the property to turn the service on.

In many cases, they can do what they need to do from outside of the property, but you or your landlord may need to meet them there to turn service on, depending on how it's set up. Your utility company should give you instructions on whether someone needs to be there or not.

Second, you will need as much time as possible to get utilities set up. Usually, they can come out within a week, but it can take longer—up to a month in some places. Because you want to make sure you have service when you move in, get this process started right away to ensure you don't end up without something essential.

CHOOSING AMONG MULTIPLE UTILITY PROVIDERS

There are some parts of the country where the resident can choose which companies to use for utilities (we see you, Texans!).

In these regions, you will have to do a little research about your options, and it can help to talk to folks who are already in the area to understand what they've selected. The range of options can be extensive, so we've put together a guide at Dwellsy.com/blog/utilitieschoice, which should be a good starting place.

Here are a few of the things you'll want to consider as you're looking over providers for your various utilities:

- **Your needs.** Consider which utilities you actually need and how much you use them. For instance, maybe you don't need a cable provider because you're okay just watching Netflix. And maybe your new rental means a switch from gas to electricity, or even to solar. Then there's your usage to consider as well: maybe your water bill tends to be high because you take long showers, or your electricity usage soars over the holidays because of your decorations. Analyzing your past spending patterns will help with this. By doing so, you'll understand exactly what you need and what kind of contracts will work best for you.
- **The provider's reputation.** The last thing you want is an unreliable utilities provider, so be sure to do your research. Reading reviews online and talking to your neighbors can both be helpful ways to get perspectives on which utility providers in your area are the best and if there are any good deals to be had.
- **The rate.** Of course, you'll want to understand what each company's rate is and compare the companies to one another. When there's a choice of utilities in an area, rates tend to be quite competitive, and this can benefit you if you do your research. This will help you understand what your bills will look like, too, so that you're not caught by surprise the first time you have to pay your utilities on top of your rent.

- **The length of the contract.** Make sure that the plan you choose aligns with the length of your lease and your budget.

SETTING UP INTERNET AND CABLE

Internet and cable are a little different because, unlike utilities, in almost all markets you have some measure of choice.

Sometimes the choice is between different companies, and sometimes it's between options at a single company.

Again, it's a good idea to start with your landlord. They should know which companies already provide service to the building, which are usually the easiest options for setup.

Usually, you have the choice of getting internet and cable service from the local legacy cable company, which, depending on your region, could be a company like AT&T, Comcast, Spectrum, or Charter. Or you could get service from the legacy local landline telephone companies, like AT&T, Verizon, and CenturyLink.

There are various satellite companies that might be attractive options for you (particularly if you're in a rural area), but make sure you talk to your landlord about the installation of a satellite dish, since they're likely to have an opinion about if and where you can install one.

In some parts of the country, you may have other companies to choose from with different types of service available.

Fiber providers can be very attractive for those who want super-fast (gig-speed) internet. It can be difficult to get these options at individual homes or small apartment complexes, but many large apartment complexes have one as an option. Sometimes this is an option from the legacy cable company, and sometimes there's a dedicated company like Google that offers the service.

With the advent of 5G service, mobile internet might be a good option for you if 5G service is strong in your area. This service isn't attached to a property, so you can bring it with you when you move, and some services provide speeds of up to one gigabit per second. These are usually available from cell-phone companies like AT&T, Verizon, and T-Mobile.

Another option is "line-of-sight internet," which is a relatively new and often inexpensive option. Its name explains how it works: buildings within the line of sight of a "mast" (a big, tall tower) can receive internet from that mast. Because the signal is wireless, it involves a lot less setup than other options. It can be very fast and dependable but is currently only available in select areas of the country.

If you're moving into a large apartment complex, it'll usually have two or three choices available, and you will need to select from those options. In some cases, it may have cut a deal with a particular internet provider to provide service to every apartment in the complex, and you would just pay your share of the overall complex fee. While you don't get to make a choice for yourself in this scenario, this approach almost always means lower-cost internet for you. If this is the case, it might be quickest and most convenient to just go with the building's Wi-Fi.

It's important to note that in February 2022, the Federal Communications Commission banned apartment-building owners from making exclusive agreements with particular internet providers. Building owners also can't split revenue with these companies, which was commonly part of these exclusive agreements. This means that you should have some choice when it comes to picking an internet-service provider. You can't have any service provider you want, because your options are still limited by the particular providers who service your area, but you've got more than one option. You can decide to go with the building's internet or choose another option that is better for you. When you're considering which provider to use, you should take into account the factors we discussed above: what kind of internet would suit your needs best, what you can afford, and what's available in your area.

DWELLSY CAN HELP

Yes, setting up utilities in your new place can be complicated. Because so many folks struggle to figure all this out, Dwellsy has partnerships with companies that can provide you with a single stop to get your whole utilities checklist done. Check out Dwellsy.com/blog/moving for all the details.

Remember: Start lining up your utilities as soon as you get your new place locked in, and don't hesitate to ask your new landlord for help.

4.2

RENTERS INSURANCE

It's important to plan for emergencies. One easy way to do so is buying renters insurance. Maybe you've never had to buy any kind of insurance before. That's okay. We're going to explain everything, from what renters insurance covers to how you can get on a plan.

WHAT IS RENTERS INSURANCE?

Renters insurance is a type of property insurance that covers your personal belongings, liabilities, and living expenses in case of a loss. It's sometimes confused with the property insurance landlords have for their buildings, but your landlord's insurance won't help you if something happens to your unit. It only covers the structure of the building, not your personal property as a renter. That's why renters insurance is important: it's for *your* stuff, not your landlord's. Standard renters insurance policies are called HO-4 policies.

DO YOU REALLY NEED RENTERS INSURANCE?

"But I plan to be really careful," you think. "I don't know if I really need renters insurance." It's true; you can cut down on a lot of different kinds of danger by being a careful tenant. You can't plan for everything, though. You can't control what your neighbors do or who comes into your building. You also can't control whether there's a fire or whether the pipes burst and flood your apartment. Any of these things could happen! Renters insurance will make sure you're ready for emergencies like these.

Renters insurance also tends to be pretty cheap and easy to get—qualities that are hard to come by in the world of insurance. This makes it a smart investment. You'll sleep better at night knowing your stuff is insured.

We'd be remiss if we didn't tell you that some landlords and some cities require renters insurance. In those places, it's just about finding the insurance that's right for you, not whether or not you buy it.

TWO TYPES OF RENTERS INSURANCE

When you go to find renters insurance, you'll generally find two types being offered: Liability Only and Liability + Personal Property.

Liability Only policies essentially protect your landlord's property against damage you might cause to it—you are protecting yourself from any "liability" you may face.

Liability + Personal Property (generally referred to as HO-4 insurance) will include liability insurance as well as coverage of your personal stuff and potentially some other things. What other things? Read on . . .

WHAT RENTERS INSURANCE WILL COVER

Okay, so let's talk specifics. What does renters insurance actually cover? It will vary from policy to policy, but here's what a standard HO-4 renters-insurance policy normally covers:

- **Personal property.** Yep, it covers your stuff. By this, we mean clothing, jewelry, electronics, furniture, any collections that you might have (vinyl, books, DVDs), and all kinds of other things. Your belongings will be covered whether you're at home or away, although the coverage might be limited if you're away. (For example, if your bike is stolen outside a shop, renters insurance might cover it.)
- **Loss of use.** If your home becomes uninhabitable through a disaster that your insurance covers, you will often be covered for expenses like hotel bills and restaurant food while your home is being repaired.
- **Liability coverage.** This comes in handy if a third party files a lawsuit against you because of injury or damage that took place in your rental. Without liability coverage, you'd have to cover all of the legal expenses yourself, and those can be super expensive. Renters insurance will also provide coverage if you or another tenant cause injury to someone else, like if your dog bites a guest. (Note that certain dog breeds are excluded from most renters-insurance policies, so if you have a dog, make sure to ask an insurance agent whether your pet is covered.)
- **Medical expenses.** Like liability coverage, medical coverage also applies if someone sustains an injury on your property. However, medical coverage comes into effect regardless of who is at fault for the injury, whereas liability coverage is only applicable if you are at fault.

DISASTERS COVERED BY RENTERS INSURANCE

Not all disasters are covered under renters insurance. Here are the ones that are most commonly covered:

- Explosion
- Windstorm or hail
- Fire

- Civil commotion or riot
- Damage by vehicles
- Damage by aircraft
- Vandalism or malicious mischief
- Smoke
- Theft
- Volcanic eruption
- Weight of snow, ice, or sleet
- Falling object
- Freezing of household appliances or systems
- Accidental release of steam or water from certain household appliances or systems
- Unintentional and sudden tearing apart, burning, cracking, or bulging of certain household systems
- Accidental or sudden damage from artificially generated electric currents

WHAT RENTERS INSURANCE WILL NOT COVER

There are lots of things renters insurance will not cover. Most of these are referred to as "acts of God," such as earthquakes, floods, and sewage backup into your apartment. If you live in an area where you're at risk of these things, you can pay to have coverage added on. You might also have to purchase other insurance to cover particularly expensive items.

Renters insurance also may not cover damage or theft caused by your own negligence, such as not locking your door or leaving your bath running so that it overflows. This includes intentional acts as well.

If you have super-expensive stuff like an engagement ring or an art collection (who has an art collection?!), it's also usually not included without additional coverage.

ADD-ONS FOR RENTERS INSURANCE

If a regular renters-insurance policy doesn't cover everything you would like it to, you can purchase add-ons. Here are a few of the most common customizations and how they can help insure you more fully:

- **Replacement-cost coverage.** Regular renters insurance will replace your possessions for their actual value. For instance, say your ten-year-old couch is ruined when your bathroom floods. You'd get a check from your renters-insurance company that would cover the cost of a used couch. Of course, you won't want another ten-year-old couch—you'll want a new one. Replacement-cost coverage will ensure that your possessions will be valued as if they were new. So, with this add-on, you'd get enough money to buy a new couch.
- **Scheduled personal property.** If you have some unusually expensive things, like jewelry or high-end electronics, this is for you. Normally, renters-insurance companies put a cap on the amount that they'll compensate you. If you have belongings worth more than this cap, this add-on will allow you to have those items professionally appraised and added to your policy for an extra cost.
- **Identity-theft coverage: Some renters-insurance companies offer coverage related to identity theft.** This add-on will help with legal fees, credit monitoring, and document-replacement costs.

HOW DO YOU GET RENTERS INSURANCE?

Okay, so you've decided that you want (or need) renters insurance. Great! How do you actually go about getting it? The world of insurance might seem overwhelming, but this is actually one of the easier types to acquire. Let's walk through the process step by step.

1. **Estimate the value of your property.** Renters often underestimate the value of their property, so you want to be careful about this. Methodically go through all of your things, keep a running list of their estimated value, and then add it all up at the end. It's a good idea to note particularly expensive items in case you need to get them covered separately. This is also a good opportunity to document your property so that you have pictures if you ever need to claim their value from your insurance company.
2. **Compare insurance companies.** Once you have a good estimate of the value of your belongings, you can start actually looking for insurance companies. There are a number of ways to find an insurance company; we have a site (Dwellsy.com/blog/rentersinsurance) that can help you find specific options for renters insurance, or you can ask family and friends for recommendations. Maybe you already have an insurance company you trust because you have auto insurance or something similar with it, and you can use its renters insurance. (You might even save money by bundling your policies.) It's a good idea to do some research on how reputable the companies are, too—maybe the reviews online will tell you a company doesn't pay when a claim is made.
3. **Apply for insurance.** The next step is to apply. This should be a simple process, and it's likely you can do the whole thing online. There might be some questions about your building that you don't immediately know the answers to, like the year it was built, but you can ask your landlord about those. If you like a bunch of different insurance companies, apply to all of them. You can pick the one that offers you the best deal in the end. When it comes time to decide your deductible, think carefully, and remember that the premium will be higher if your deductible is lower.
4. **Consider what add-ons you want.** If you want any of the add-ons we discussed earlier, you'll also have a chance to customize your policy. This will ensure that you have solid coverage.

And that's it! All that's left to do after these steps is to pay for your policy. It's often cheaper to do this annually instead of monthly because sometimes insurance companies tack on pesky administrative fees if you pay monthly. Not so bad, right?

Remember: We recommend renters insurance for most people, whether it's required or not. It's an inexpensive way to get some protection for your place and stuff.

4.3

MOVING OUT OF THE OLD AND INTO THE NEW

So your move-in date is set and you're ready to rock. All that's left is to actually do the moving itself. This can be intimidating: it's a lot of logistics and manual labor, so it's not up everyone's alley. We're here with a little advice and to walk you through some of the major points.

Don't worry—it's all going to get done, one way or another. You'll be moved in before you know it.

HOW TO GET YOUR STUFF FROM POINT A TO POINT B

The big question: How are you actually going to move your stuff? You've got two options: you can call a moving company, or you can do it yourself. You might be torn, so let's go over the pros and cons of both options.

Calling the Movers

Pros	Cons
• Less manual labor involved • Hire a good company, and it'll know what it's doing and will pack your stuff well to minimize breakage and other damage • Lowers stress (for some), which allows you to deal with the rest of your move instead of focusing on physically moving your things	• Expensive—movers can cost hundreds of dollars per hour and thousands of dollars for a full move • Less flexibility because you will have to work on the movers' schedule rather than at your own pace • They might mishandle or break your belongings

Doing It Yourself

Pros	Cons
• Cheaper—it'll probably just be the cost of a truck rental or something similar if you handle things yourself • You'll be able to work at your own pace, on your own schedule • You can pack exactly how you'd like to instead of having to seal everything up and be ready to go by the time movers come	• Lots of manual labor is involved because you'll be doing all the heavy lifting • Lots of planning—you'll have to think about both hiring a truck and how to pack it, as well as all of the other logistical issues that come with getting from Point A to Point B • Unexpected issues—you might have a couch get stuck in the door or something similar, with no one to help you fix the situation • You might break more of your own stuff than professional movers would have

Where to Find Packing Materials

Depending on whether you have movers or opt to DIY your move, you might need to get packing materials—boxes, tape, cushioning, and anything else you think you might need. If you splurge on full-service movers, you won't have to worry about anything, but with movers who only do the essentials, you'll have to get everything packed and sealed before they come. Most companies will have boxes available for a fee, if you'd rather do that. Of course, you'll also need various materials if you choose to do your move yourself. You have options, including the following:

- **Buying online or in a store.** You can buy boxes from many large retailers, like Amazon, Walmart, or Home Depot. These will have the benefit of being cheap, and if they need to be shipped to you, they'll come quickly. If you go to a physical store, however, you'll have the added benefit of being able to see how big the boxes are so that you can better assess how much packing material you'll need. The downside is that you might not be able to choose exactly what kinds of boxes you get or how many.
- **Moving kits.** Some retailers, like Home Depot, offer moving kits. These kits have several different sizes of boxes in different quantities, and they'll also come with padding, tape, and other packing materials. You can often customize the amount of any given box or material in the kit; that way, you'll know for sure you have enough for your home.
- **Movers' reusable containers.** Some movers provide reusable plastic containers, both for convenience and to lower your environmental impact. They bring them to you, and after your move, they'll come back and take the empties.
- **Movers' boxes for a fee.** Many movers will be able to provide you with boxes and other materials for a fee, even if you have to pack them up yourself. When you're booking your move, look into what kinds of boxes and materials are available and what the cost will be. Then, you can compare this option with your other options to decide what makes the most sense.

LOCAL VS. LONG-DISTANCE MOVES

Distance matters when you're moving, especially if you're going to call the movers.

If you're moving a long distance—to another state, let's say—you might have trouble finding a moving company willing to help you out. You'll want to do your research carefully and make sure you pick a company that can travel the necessary distance. Interstate movers have to carry extra paperwork: both a license from the Federal Motor Carrier Safety Administration and the correct insurance. This is part of why these movers are harder to come by.

Interstate moves are also typically more expensive. It's not uncommon for interstate moves to cost many thousands of dollars. That's another thing you'll have to budget for if you call the movers.

If you make a long move yourself, the number-one thing you're going to want to do is be careful when you estimate the amount of stuff you have. You want to be certain to rent the right truck size so that everything will fit. It can be easy to underestimate the amount of stuff you're bringing, so be sure to overestimate a little instead. During a short move, you can always go back for your other things, but that's not the case if you're traveling a very long distance. Just be careful!

You also have an in-between option: you can hire movers at both ends—one group to pack your stuff up and get it into a vehicle, and another group to move stuff into your new place and get it unpacked. You just have to do the driving in the middle. In essence, how involved you want to be is totally up to you.

PACK A BOX OF MOVE-IN ESSENTIALS

You'll want to pack an easy-to-reach box of essentials to keep with you during the move. This can be an easy thing to forget once you're caught up in the hustle and bustle of the move, but it will save you a lot of hassle. No one wants to be digging through boxes for their pajamas on their first night in a new place, right?

Here's what you'll want to consider packing in your move-in box:

- **An overnight bag.** This is probably the most important thing on this list. Chances are your overnight stuff will be spread throughout a few boxes. Having your pajamas, toothbrush, moisturizer, and whatever else in one place will save you from having to hunt around.
- **Bedding and pillows.** When you're tired and achy from unpacking, the last thing you want to do is unearth your bedding from all of your stuff. Keeping your bedding close at hand means that all you'll have to do is make your bed.
- **Cleaning supplies.** You may want to do some cleaning as soon as you get there—the situation could be a little dusty. This way, you can get started on the first day if you'd like to.
- **A tool kit.** Obviously, everything in your new rental should be in top shape. If anything does happen to need a minor repair, though, or if you want to do some furniture reassembly, you'll be ready if you have a tool kit at hand. Just throw a small toolbox into your box of essentials, and you'll be prepared right off the bat.
- **A first aid kit.** There's quite a bit of manual labor involved in moving, especially if you do it yourself. If anyone gets a cut or scrape, you'll be ready with your handy first aid kit.
- **Toilet paper and paper towels.** Don't get caught moving into your new apartment and having to go when . . . there's no TP. Eating pizza with no napkins is bound to make a mess of your immaculate new place, too.
- **A speaker.** Don't underestimate the power of music! Nothing can lift tired spirits more than some good bops. Be prepared for an unpacking dance party!
- **Snacks and water.** Moving is thirsty work! You'll be glad to have a big bottle of water nearby once you've flopped down on the floor after hauling up your mattress. Some fun snacks to fortify you will get you all energized so that you can tackle the next box.
- **Books, gaming devices, and other entertainment.** Once you're ready to unwind for the night, you're going to want your favorite

book or your Nintendo Switch to curl up with. Having a few of your favorite things to do in the box will be a nice treat for when you're done with the first day of moving, especially if friends are helping you.

BEFORE YOU LEAVE

Once you're all packed up for the move, there are still a few things left to do before you head out:

- **Do a deep-clean.** You'll be expected to return your old unit to your landlord in the same condition it was in when you began your tenancy. This means that either you'll have to deep-clean the place yourself or you should hire a cleaning company to help you. Either way, you'll want to make sure that your rental is in tip-top shape before you leave; otherwise, your landlord will likely use part of your security deposit to pay for a cleaning service.
- **Do a final walkthrough.** Make sure to schedule a time for your landlord to walk through your rental just before you leave so that you can be certain there are no problems with the condition you've left the rental in. If there are, you can work out a solution with your landlord then and there rather than having them take a chunk out of your security deposit.
- **Get your security deposit back.** Make sure that you ask for your security deposit back! If your landlord can't give it to you before you leave, then make sure to leave them your forwarding address or another kind of payment information. (More on this in Section 5.4).
- **Return your keys.** Hand in your keys! If you don't, your landlord might use part of your security deposit to change the locks.

THE FIRST THING TO DO ONCE YOU GET THERE

You've arrived at your new place, you've got the keys, and now it's all yours! You probably want to get it ready and start unpacking, but there's something you need to do first—take pictures.

Why take pictures? Because it's the first step to getting your security deposit back later. Documenting the exact condition of the rental at the time you moved in will settle any disputes that may arise later on about whether or not you have damaged the place.

Walk the whole space, inside and out, and take photos or videos of everything, especially anything that shows damage or existing wear and tear.

Then, send those photos (or a video) to the landlord to make sure they're on the same page and have the same information you have.

Once that's done, check the end date of your lease and set a calendar reminder for 120 days before that date so you can be reminded to figure out whether to stay in your rental or move. Your future self will thank you.

TIME TO CLEAN!

We know that when you're moving, the last thing you want to think about is cleaning. But the thing is, it'll be a lot easier to give the apartment an initial scrub-down before all of your stuff is unpacked and in the way. By giving the place a quick clean before you unpack, you'll be doing yourself a huge favor. Here are the things we think are most essential to clean before unpacking:

- **The fridge.** If you brought perishable food with you, you'll want to store it right away, so it's essential to have a clean fridge. Even if you didn't bring groceries, you'll probably be buying some soon, and you'll need a clean place to put them. Because the fridge will be empty, taking out and cleaning the shelves should be a pretty simple job. You'll be done before you know it.

- **The rest of the kitchen.** Once you've finished the fridge, you can move on to the rest of the kitchen. You want clean cabinets to store the rest of your food and the things you use to eat with, like your cutlery and plates. Clean from top to bottom: do the light fixtures and the tops of the cabinets, then move on to the countertops and the appliances. You can do the floors later.
- **The bathrooms.** You can follow the same top-to-bottom approach when you deal with the bathrooms. Deal with the showerhead and upper walls, and then you can move on to the counter surfaces, the sink, and the shower floor. With the bathroom in particular, you'll want to focus on disinfecting as much as on making the place look nice. This means being particularly careful with places like the shower and the toilet.
- **The rest.** Follow the same top-down strategy for the remaining rooms. Start with the ceilings, light fixtures, tops of doors, and anything else up high. Then you can do tables, windows, and other mid-level surfaces. Lastly, you'll want to finish with all of the floors.

CHOOSE THE BEST ORDER TO UNPACK ROOMS

We know that it can be tempting to just wing it and start unpacking boxes at random. However, things will get done a lot more quickly if there's some method to your madness. Here's our suggested order of how to unpack your rooms:

- **The bedroom.** Once you start unpacking, the first thing you want to do is make your bed. It might sound a little crazy, but we promise it'll end up making sense. Think about it: after unpacking all of those other boxes, are you really going to want to make your bed? You'd rather just fall into it, right? You'll thank yourself at the end of the day. While you're at it, you can go ahead and get the rest of the bedroom unpacked. It'll be your oasis of calm in the madness.

- **The kitchen.** Get your food sorted out and into the fridge if it needs to go there. On your first day, take the time to at least make sure the basic appliances are there: the coffee maker, the toaster, and the other things you need to make breakfast without too much of a hassle. There's always time to go back and organize it to your liking later.
- **The bathroom.** This won't take very long, and it'll be convenient for you to have your bathroom all set up. Go ahead and put away all of your products and medicines where they need to be so that you're ready for your usual routines the first night and the following morning.
- **The living area.** You can take longer unpacking the living room. Get the furniture organized just how you'd like it to be, shift the lamps and tables around, all of that. There'll be time to put your pictures and decorations up later on as you continue to settle in.

Remember: Cleaning and packing can be overwhelming. Break it into small chunks to make it more manageable.

4.4

CHANGING YOUR ADDRESS

Changing your address sucks. No two ways about it. Every time we've ever moved, we've always been surprised by how many places there are where we have to change it.

If you want to do it on your own, the starting point is the US Postal Service (USPS), which has an address-changing tool that can change your address with the post office and set up a forwarding service to have all your old mail forwarded to your new address.

With that done, you can reach out to any other known places that have your address and change it with them. It's often helpful to look through every piece of mail you receive at your current address and identify ones that you want to make sure have your new address. Here are a few places you should update with your new address:

- Your job
- Tax agencies
- Social Security Administration
- Phone, cable, and internet services
- Gas and electricity providers

- Insurance providers—including renters-insurance providers
- Subscriptions, such as magazines or food kits
- Department of Motor Vehicles
- Bank/credit union, Paypal, Venmo
- Credit cards
- Google Maps, Apple Maps, autofill addresses
- Rideshare apps like Uber and Lyft
- Voter registration
- All of your doctors and your dentist
- Lawyers and accountants

When you move into your new address, keep an eye on all the items that are forwarded to you and, within a month or so, send your updated address to those places.

There is a shortcut available, if you like shortcuts. There are address-changing services out there, and Dwellsy has figured out how to bring them to you for free. These services can change your address with the USPS and can help you identify any other places where your address needs to be changed—and change your address for you with them. You can find these options at Dwellsy.com/blog/moving.

Remember: If you can, sit down and get it all done in one go. Then you won't have to worry about it later!

4.5

A BRIEF MOVE-IN CHECKLIST

We just threw a lot of information at you about what you'll need to do when you move in, so let's break it down into a short, friendly checklist. This is just for reference; if you want more detail, you can go back through past sections for exactly what you need.

1. Set a move-in date and book movers if necessary. Alert friends, family, and your employer about your upcoming move.
2. Gather packing materials, if necessary, and pack up your items.
3. Find out who is responsible for what utilities and ensure that they will be running when you move in. Also ensure that they'll be transferred into your name when you move. If you need to make a choice between providers, do so.
4. Make sure that all relevant people and institutions know about your upcoming address change. In some cases, you may not be able to change your address until you've actually moved into your new place—that's okay! Make a note to do it later.
5. Do a final deep-clean. Then, do a walkthrough of your old place with your landlord to make sure everything looks right.

6. Move out and into your new home! Make sure to either collect your security deposit from your old landlord on your way out or leave them with your new address so they can send you a check.
7. Set a reminder on your phone for 120 days before your next lease end date as soon as you move in—you'll thank yourself later.
8. Deep-clean the new place and start to unpack. Take out your box of move-in essentials first so that you have it nearby. Remember to take pictures of the place's condition.
9. Start your life in your new place!

So now that we've talked through the logistical facets of moving, let's move on to a more emotional part of the process. We're going to discuss your relationships with the people around you at your new place.

4.6

RELATIONSHIPS: LANDLORDS, NEIGHBORS, AND ROOMMATES

During the day-to-day life of your tenancy, you'll find that you're building plenty of new relationships with the people around you.

These relationships can be essential to having a good rental experience—the last thing you want is to have endless friction with someone you see every day.

That's why we're going to provide you with some of our best tips for dealing with some of the most important relationships in your life as a renter: your landlord, your roommate, and your neighbors.

LANDLORD

Hopefully, you already have a little bit of a relationship with your landlord and the landlord team (leasing staff, maintenance team, etc.) from when you applied for the rental. You want to make sure that you keep things professional and polite throughout the duration of your tenancy.

Here are a few things you can do to make sure that your relationship is smooth sailing:

Be polite and communicative. Politeness can go a long way. Assuming you've done your best to keep things courteous during the application process, keep it up. You want your landlord to understand that you respect them. This includes making sure to communicate with your landlord when something goes wrong, like required maintenance or late rent. They'll appreciate the heads-up, and it'll make you look good.

Pay rent as promptly as you can. Paying rent on time is a key part of your relationship with your landlord. You want to make sure that you're keeping up your part of the bargain, which means paying your rent in full at the agreed time. Setting up autopay with your bank is a great option to make sure you don't have to remember to make the payment. If you know you can't pay on time, make sure to give your landlord as much of a warning as you can.

You may not be thinking about this, but in most cases, your landlord needs your rent in order to turn around and pay their mortgage, insurance, or other bills associated with your property. If you're late on the rent, they might need to be late on the mortgage. Getting them in hot water with their bank is not going to help your relationship with them, that's for sure.

Take good care of the property. The better you take care of their property, the more your landlord will appreciate you as a tenant. They're certain to notice if you're letting the place fall apart or keeping it constantly dirty, even if you think they have no idea. This includes letting your landlord know as soon as something is broken or if you have pests or mold. The sooner they know, the sooner the issue will be fixed without getting much worse.

Give as much notice as possible when you plan to move out. Your unit is part of your landlord's income, so it's important that they're able to line up a new tenant before you move out. Empty units can cost a landlord lots of money, so they'll appreciate having as much notice as you can give them to avoid vacancy being an issue.

ROOMMATES

Maybe your roommate was your best friend before you moved in. Maybe you just met them, and you're getting to know them. Regardless, you're probably sharing space more intimately than you've done with anyone but your parents and siblings, so some ground rules for how you'll occupy the space make a ton of sense.

Communicate as much as possible. Communication is key to a healthy roommate relationship. Annoyed about the dirty dishes in the sink? Express it kindly and politely. Wondering if you can split rent a different way? Bring it up in conversation. The earlier and more polite and respectful you are, the better things will go. You should be able to expect the same from a good roommate.

Write a roommate agreement. We're big fans of writing roommate agreements—signed contracts that lay out all of your ground rules. It helps to have something in writing to refer back to when you have a disagreement, just in case someone misremembers what you agreed to. That way, everyone will always be clear on what the rules are, and they can hold themselves and others accountable to them. The details on these are in Section 3.2, so head there if you need a refresher.

Keep your expectations realistic. Your roommates are just as human as you are. They might be messy, loud, or down in the dumps sometimes. You'll never have a roommate who's perfect all of the time. Try to give them a little leeway, and hopefully they'll do the same for you.

Be friendly to their friends and family. It's awful to bring a guest to your apartment and have someone who lives there give you the cold shoulder. Your roommate will like you more if you're kind to the people they bring around. Even just a smile and a "Hi, how are you doing?" can go a long way.

NEIGHBORS

Ah, neighbors. The source of so many potential lifelong friends or frenemies and full-on enemies if things are handled badly. So much about getting along with neighbors comes down to respect and boundaries.

Be mindful of the noise you make. We've talked a little bit about this, but it bears repeating: try to be conscious of your own noise level. If you know things might be a little loud, like if you're planning a party, let your neighbors know so that they're not caught by surprise. It'll probably avoid a noise complaint.

If you have a complaint, make it civil. So, what if your neighbors are the loud ones? If you have a reason to complain to your neighbors, be sure to keep things polite. Being kind will often make people more willing to listen than if you're angry or aggressive. Even if something is wrong, it doesn't necessarily need to turn into a conflict or a confrontation.

Greet people when you run into them. You don't need to say a lot—just "Hi, how are you?" works here, too. It's just nice to acknowledge people, and they'll appreciate it, too. It might make them more willing to listen if you ever need a favor or lodge a complaint with them. You want to do everything you can to humanize the people around you, even if you don't interact with them otherwise.

Do favors if you can. If you're able, do the things that your neighbors ask of you. Pet sit their animals, watch their children for a minute, lend them a cup of sugar—whatever it is. It's kind, and you'll be in their good graces. If you ever need a favor of your own, you'll know that you can turn to them.

Help your pet be respectful, too. If you have a dog, pick up their poop and don't let them pee right in front of the door—that kills the grass and won't help you make friends.

We hope that these are useful tools to make the relationships you have with those around you as pleasant as possible!

Remember: Cultivating these relationships can pay off in the long run, whether it's during an emergency or even if you just need a favor.

4.7

WHO MAINTAINS WHAT?

You might be a little uncertain about who's supposed to take care of what in your rental apartment. There are a lot of different things that go into keeping a home in working order, and you'll want to understand what you have to do versus what's your landlord's responsibility. Let's break it down.

THE BOTTOM LINE

At a minimum, your landlord is required to keep your rental "habitable." So what makes an apartment or other dwelling habitable? There are different definitions depending on the state, so be sure to check your local laws. Generally, a dwelling must be structurally sound and free from infestation to be considered habitable. It should also have adequate water, heat, and electricity.

READ YOUR LEASE

Beyond habitability, who is responsible for which maintenance tasks in your home should be listed in your lease. You should read it carefully to understand exactly what's required of you and what your landlord will do for you. If you have any questions, talk them over with your landlord. And be sure to document the condition of your new home at move-in with pictures and/or video—following up with an email to your landlord if they do not provide a move-in form listing the conditions of the unit is a good idea, too.

Here's generally how the division of responsibilities goes:

Your Landlord Is Usually Responsible for Repairs

Landlords are often responsible for major and minor repairs around your rental. If your smoke detector isn't working or your sink won't turn on anymore, your landlord is the person you should tell. If these repairs come from normal wear and tear—as in, they're not your fault—the landlord is responsible for them and will foot the bill for the repair. If you caused the damage, you will have to pay for it to be repaired (and it will probably come out of your security deposit when you move out if you're not billed right away).

If the repair in question makes the rental "uninhabitable," your landlord is likely required to fix it within twenty-four to forty-eight hours. Check your local laws for the specifics.

Your Landlord Is Usually Responsible for Infestations

This falls under the "habitable" thing, too. If you have an insect infestation in your rental home and it is not your fault, your landlord is usually responsible for making sure that it gets sorted out. Again, check your local laws.

However, if the infestation is due to your behavior, getting rid of the infestation is your responsibility, and you'll have to pay for it. This means you'll want to be careful about keeping things tidy. There's nothing fun about an infestation.

You'll also want to make sure the pest is really an issue. If you are new to an area of the country, you might think something is an infestation when it is actually a short-lived phenomenon. For example, mosquito hawks are common in Tennessee summers, but they go away pretty quickly. Cockroaches are in nearly every New York City and Texas apartment and house. Rodents are everywhere in lots of places across the country. Cases like these are not necessarily infestations but simply the ebb and flow of natural life in these communities, and while no one necessarily loves sharing their home with uninvited guests, the landlord's probably not going to do much in one of these situations.

Your Landlord Is Usually Responsible for Yard Work and Snow Removal, but Not Always

If you're living in a house or a townhouse, there might be questions about who takes care of what in terms of yard work and snow removal, so discuss these with your landlord. (Local laws will regulate this, too.) In most apartment buildings, however, these things are the landlord's responsibility and part of the entire building's maintenance.

You Are Usually Responsible for Smaller Maintenance Tasks

You'll have to do a bunch of smaller maintenance tasks around your rental to keep the place shipshape. These tasks include changing the lightbulbs, changing the air filters, taking out the trash, using the appliances correctly, and keeping the place relatively clean. Read the lease to find out exactly what you have to do. It's important to follow these rules because, otherwise, your landlord might take a chunk out of your security deposit.

KEEP YOUR EXPECTATIONS REALISTIC

Bear in mind that in owner-operated rentals, the number of repairs and how you handle your requests can be the difference between a landlord breaking even or losing money. If you're respectful of the unit and the property, landlords will do a lot to keep you as a tenant. However, if you have unrealistic expectations, they will breathe a sigh of relief the day you move out.

For example, if you're moving into a hundred-year-old home, everything probably won't function as well as it would in a brand-new luxury condo. It's a good idea to keep that in mind after you move in. Reasonable expectations will help you form a happy, healthy relationship with your landlord.

If you're unhappy with the way maintenance is divided, talk to your landlord. It's possible the two of you can work something out together.

Remember: No matter where you live, there's always maintenance to be done. Make sure you know what's expected of you and what you can expect of your landlord.

4.8

BE READY FOR EMERGENCIES

Part of life in any home is preparing for the worst. When emergencies happen, you want to be ready to go and not have to worry about putting together the basics you need. Because emergencies can take many different forms—from fires to floods to not making rent—this section will cover some emergency basics that we hope will serve as a general aid should you ever need it. In order to feel safe and comfortable in your new rental, you'll want to be prepared as best you can for all of the different ways that things could go wrong.

There are lots of places to start in being ready for emergencies, but since we're focused on your home, we're going to start there, and that means an emergency kit.

Here are a few of the things you'll want in your kit:

- Flashlights and lanterns
- Extra sets of batteries
- First aid supplies—bandages, Neosporin, etc.
- Drinking water
- Nonperishable food

- Power bank(s) (charged up!)
- Emergency cash
- Important phone numbers—landlord's and family members' included
- Dust masks and surgical masks
- Hand sanitizer

Of course, your emergency kit can have anything in it that makes sense for you. This could include things like extra medication or baby food. Stash your kit somewhere safe but out of the way so that you'll remember where it is if you need it.

AN EMERGENCY FUND COMES IN HANDY

It's always a good idea to have a fund stashed away for any emergencies. Saving can be daunting at first, but there are a few things you can do to make saving more manageable. You might want to start by saving a minimum amount, such as $500, just to make sure you have some cash ready for those unexpected hiccups.

From there, experts suggest saving three to six months' worth of expenses. This isn't a hard-and-fast rule, but it's a good starting point. You want to make sure that you can carry yourself through a rough patch if you hit one; for instance, if you lose your job, you'll need to be able to pay your bills while you look for another one.

At the end of the day, something is better than nothing, and whatever you can save will be helpful in a pinch. Even if you can only contribute a little bit at a time, it's worth stashing away what you can. We understand that it can be hard to do, and we encourage you to use our advice in any way that is most helpful to you. Only you know your own financial situation, and you should do what you can according to it.

FACTORS TO CONSIDER IN YOUR SAVINGS PLAN

When planning for how much you'll save each month, there are a few things you'll want to consider:

- The minimum amount you need to cover your monthly expenses
- How stable your various income sources are

You'll want to be realistic about the amount that you can save from month to month, considering what you can afford to save and what will make you feel comfortable.

TIPS FOR BUILDING YOUR FUND

- **Track your income and expenses.** How much do you earn and spend in a month? Keeping track of it will help you set realistic monthly savings goals. Make sure to include recurring bills like utility and rent, as well as occasional expenses like dinners out and new clothes.
- **Set goals for your fund.** It's good to have something to work toward. For example, if you're just starting out on your fund, you can set goals for when to have your first hundred dollars saved, and then your first thousand. Setting smaller goals will make your end goal of a full emergency fund seem more attainable.
- **Contribute consistently.** It's easy to have a certain portion of your paycheck sent directly to a savings account every pay period. That way, you can be sure you're contributing to your emergency fund, and you won't even have to think about it. Any extra contributions you're able to make on top of these regular ones will help your savings account even more.

- **Monitor your progress.** You can keep a running record of how much you save, or you can opt to be notified regularly by your bank. Either way, seeing the progress of your emergency fund will encourage you to keep saving.
- **Save your tax refund.** It's tempting to want to spend your tax refund right away. If you can, though, consider popping it straight into your savings account. That'll boost your fund!
- **Keep your fund accessible.** You want to keep your emergency fund readily available because if you ever have to dip into it, you'll need the money right away. Your best option is a savings account at a bank or credit union so that you can withdraw your money right away if you need it.
- **Stick to it.** The most important thing to do when you're building an emergency fund is to stick with it. Even when you slip up, and even if the fund doesn't grow as quickly as you'd like, the only way it will grow is if you keep adding to it bit by bit. Make sure the account is separate from your regular checking account, and make sure that your goals are realistic. Keep contributing what you can, and you'll get there.

Remember: Two important takeaways here: 1) your emergency fund should suit your needs and circumstances, and 2) consistency is key.

4.9

SPRUCING UP YOUR APARTMENT

Moving on from emergencies to a more pleasant topic: let's talk about how to make your rental apartment feel like a home. This can be difficult because landlords will place limitations on the kinds of changes you can make to your apartment. The last thing you want to do is put your security deposit in jeopardy or have to pay even more at move-out if the costs of reverting your changes are higher than the deposit!

Not to worry! We have plenty of ideas for simple ways you can add a personal touch to your apartment, and they'll all be easy to remove once your tenancy comes to an end.

MAKING YOUR APARTMENT FEEL LIKE HOME

Turning your rental into a place that really feels like "you" can seem like a daunting task, but with a few simple upgrades, it'll be easy.

- **Cleanliness.** The more quickly you're able to get your place organized, the faster it will feel like home. When you're getting unpacked, try keeping an open trash bag nearby so that trash doesn't build up on the floor or tables. From there, it will be easier for you to begin to set out appliances, picture frames, and other such things exactly where you would like them.

- **Comfort and softness.** We mentioned that before you do anything else in your new rental, you should make your bed. Eventually, you might also want to set some blankets out on the couch, if you have one. Nothing will make your place feel like home more than a Netflix session or a nap, and you need all the comfies and cozies to do that.
- **Mementos.** Even if you don't know exactly where they should go yet, set up a few picture frames or knickknacks. It'll make the place seem more like home while you're getting everything else set up. You can always move them later.
- **Light.** Lighting can have a huge impact on your mood. Think about how jarring harsh overhead lights can be or how pleasant the cheerful glow of fairy lights is. What do you want your apartment to feel like? Thoughtfully consider your lighting situation, and you can change the whole vibe of your apartment.
- **Smell.** You might not think the smell of your new place matters unless it's actively bothering you. Smell is important, though—it has a strong connection to memory. In order to make your rental feel like home, you want to make sure it smells like home. Even a few spritzes of an air freshener can make a big difference. Wall-plug scents are a great option, but be wary of candles, which often leave residual soot that can be very difficult to clean up, not to mention the fire risk. Or you could even bake cookies! It might seem like a little thing, but filling your space with your favorite scents could end up making a big difference.
- **Music.** Play some tunes while you get unpacked. It's nice to let a song you love fill the air of your new place, turning the strange into the familiar. You can also use the music as an excuse to break in your rental by having a little dance party. Just be mindful of the neighbors.

- **Getting to know your neighbors.** And speaking of neighbors, they can help you turn your rental into a home, too! You'll be more comfortable once you know the people in the apartments around you. It's worth stopping when you see someone to introduce yourself. Friendly faces are a part of making a home, too. You might gain a few friendly tips about the building or neighborhood and maybe even receive some offers to help you move in.

EASY AESTHETIC TOUCHES

There are a few other aesthetic touches you can make to your rental to spruce it up a little. Here are our best renter-friendly suggestions:

- **Peel-and-stick wallpaper.** This is an easy way to customize your rental's look without any permanent damage to your walls. Because removable wallpaper is growing more and more popular, there are lots of different designs out there. You can choose one that suits you best. If there's any residue from the wallpaper when you take it down, you should be able to clean it off easily with soapy water or adhesive remover.
- **Tile tattoos.** Tile tattoos are stickers that go over your tiles to add a more interesting pattern. If you have some dreary tiled walls or an older kitchen, these will help to spice up the situation a little. They're easy to apply—they really are just like stickers in that sense—and they'll be easy to remove once you need to take them off.
- **Washi tape.** Washi tape is a type of masking tape, normally covered with a color or pattern. It's perfect as a decorative choice for your rental because it won't cause damage to your walls or leave any residue. You can cut strips of it to create different patterns or use it to accent your pictures and posters.
- **Plants.** It's nice to have a few green, growing things. Plants have a way of making a space more homey just by being around.

- **Throw pillows.** Who doesn't love a pillow or two? Plus, it's fun to pick ones that match with your furniture. Toss a few onto your couch, and you might be surprised at the effect they have.
- **Bamboo blinds.** Tons of blinds are a bland, impersonal white. Why not try some bamboo blinds to give your space a little more personality? They're easy to install, clean, and maintain, so you won't have to worry about all of the upkeep. They're an easy touch that will complement any other natural elements of your apartment nicely.
- **Framed posters and paintings.** If you've got a ton of leftover posters and pictures from high school or college and you want to keep them around, it's a good idea to get them framed. They'll look classier that way. Big posters or art pieces are a great way to take up extra space on a wall. If you want some art but don't want to pay big bucks for an expensive piece by someone famous, you could consider looking for a local artist instead. Street fairs are great for this kind of thing. You get cool art, the artist gets paid to make cool art, and the local economy gets a boost. Everyone wins!

GO BIG (WITH YOUR LANDLORD'S COOPERATION)

In some cases, it makes sense to do more than just surface improvements to your place. This is definitely something you can do, but you'll need to involve your landlord.

You should involve them, not just because it's their property (and you kind of have to), but also because they *might pay for part or all of something you want*.

What are some of the things that you could potentially ask for, and when should you ask for them?

At Move-In

When you first move into a place, your landlord understands that there are some things you might want to do to make the place your own, and they could be in a great position to help you with those things. Depending on the type of landlord and property, they could have on-staff maintenance folks who could do some work on your unit.

Here are some upgrade options that are a little more significant that your landlord might consider right after you move in:

- **An accent wall.** Painting one wall a high-impact color can give your place Instagram-ready visual impact and help make it your own. This is the kind of thing you could do yourself, or your landlord may be able to do this for you. Usually, you're responsible for returning it to the original color before you move out, or your landlord may do that for you at your cost.
- **Appliance upgrades.** No dishwasher? Super-old appliances? Your landlord will be well aware that new appliances can increase the amount of rent they get in the long term. The challenge for them is that you're already living there, so they can't get the extra rent from you unless you're willing to offer that. You can help them with the decision by offering to pay for a part of the new appliances or by agreeing to increased rent as a result of the new appliances.
- **New carpet.** Your landlord should know that the carpet needs to be replaced every four to seven years, but maybe that didn't get done before you moved in and your carpet is looking a little sad. Like the appliance upgrades, new carpet is a fairly expensive item, but while you might need to share the cost with your landlord, it may be worth it to you. You could even ask for hardwood or hardwood-like flooring, which is more expensive but much more durable.
- **New light fixtures and ceiling fans.** These have a surprising impact on the overall vibe of your space, especially when you consider all of the different types of light out there. Maybe your current lighting situation is harsh and bright, and you'd like

something more mellow. Maybe the fixtures are old-fashioned or the fan is painted a weird color. If that's the case, you can talk to your landlord and suggest these changes. As with the other suggestions, your landlord might ask you to help cover the cost.

On Renewal

Renewing your lease is a great time to talk to the landlord about a bunch of potential upgrades. Maybe it's just time for a new coat of paint or new flooring, or maybe there's something that's really going to make your place look amazing.

Negotiating for whatever you may want at the time of renewal is great timing because your landlord's alternative to you renewing is vacancy or turnover (expensive for them) and because if they really invest to upgrade the place, you can talk about implications for the rent for the new lease, and you can make a conscious decision to trade higher rent for more improvements. Either way, as your lease is coming to an end, if you're thinking about renewing, it's a great time to think about improvements you might want that your landlord wouldn't ordinarily consider.

Part of what you should discuss with your landlord is whether or not you'll undo your upgrades at the end of your lease. If you make your own upgrades, as opposed to the landlord paying for them, the landlord might want to keep them beyond the end of your lease. This means you can use your upgrades as a negotiating tool. Since you improved the apartment and your landlord likes the improvements, there might be something in it for you—lower rent, free parking, or some other form of compensation. Otherwise, you should consider undoing your upgrades at the end of your lease to restore the unit back to its original condition. In order to make everything as clear as possible, make sure you reach an agreement with your landlord and get it in writing.

Remember: You can upgrade your rental and make it your own. And you don't have to pay big bucks to make your place look nice. Small touches can make a big difference.

4.10

FURNISHING YOUR PLACE (ON A BUDGET)

If your rental apartment is unfurnished, it can be a pain to have to furnish it yourself. Even if you split the cost of furniture with a roommate, the price might make you flinch a little—especially after paying all of your moving costs. We have a few tips to help you out with furnishing.

- **Rent furniture.** Since you're renting your apartment, it might make sense to rent the furniture as well. Depending on the duration of your lease and your lifestyle, renting can be a cost-effective option. You'll just want to be careful if you're someone with pets because if they mess up the furniture, you'll likely be on the hook for it. There's a whole new crop of furniture-rental companies out there, and many have pretty great stuff. Check out Dwellsy.com/blog/furniturerental for options.
- **Look out for garage sales.** You might spot garage sales around your community. Furniture at these will often be cheap. If you spend some time poking around at them, you might find a great deal on a couch or something that would otherwise be pretty expensive if purchased new.

- **Use Facebook Marketplace or local free-and-for-sale groups.** Yes, we know Facebook's not exactly *en vogue* at the moment, but it can be useful for stuff like this. You could score some free or cheap furniture just by scrolling Facebook Marketplace or joining some of your local free-and-for-sale groups. You might have to pick it up yourself, but hey, maybe the price will make the effort worth it.
- **Visit furniture outlet stores.** Outlet stores will have furniture and other items available at discounted prices. You might notice nicks or dents on many of these items, which is why they're being sold at a much lower price. If you're okay with those types of things, these stores are a great option for getting some furniture on a budget.
- **Know when to buy.** Winter clothing goes on sale after the winter holidays because stores start thinking about getting rid of their winter stock. Furniture stores have times of year when there are discounts, too. To get the best deals, you'll want to hit them around the end of the winter (January and February) or the end of summer (August and September). Shopping at the right time could save you a ton of money.
- **Look out for furniture your neighbors are throwing away.** Yes, your curb might provide your next piece of furniture. Tons of people throw away perfectly good stuff—why not take it home if you see something you like? It's free! Make sure to clean it well, and you'll be golden.
- **Think about the essentials.** Figure out your basics, buy those, and then go from there. Your essentials will probably be stuff like a bed, couch, dining table, and chair. Once you've got all the things you really need, you can see how much is left in your budget for extras. You don't want to overspend on things you don't need, especially because you might have to find ways to get rid of those items if you move again and they don't suit or fit in your next place.

It's a good idea to remember that if you own your furniture (instead of renting it), you can change it to suit your liking. Get crafty and paint it a new color. Combine it with other pieces of furniture or take it apart. It's all up to you!

Remember: The amount of people giving cool furniture away for free online is amazing. Make use of that (safely).

4.11

PESTS & CREEPY-CRAWLIES

Just mention a cockroach or a mouse, and you'll see many faces twist in disgust. Pests are truly one of the worst parts of living in a home or apartment. You might get lucky and never have to deal with them, but you don't want to live in fear of an infestation. In this section, we're going to talk you through some of the most common pests, how to prevent them, and how to get rid of them if you have them.

Before we talk about different kinds of pests, we want to mention that the solutions we offer are only for small-scale problems. Many pests reproduce quickly, so you could have an infestation on your hands before you know it. If you think you're experiencing an infestation, please contact your landlord, who will call an extermination company. An infestation isn't something you should handle yourself; the experts will be able to help you out.

Also, most pests are attracted to messes, particularly food messes. One of the best ways to avoid any infestation before it happens is to keep your food up and away from the ground in secure containers and to keep the counters and sink clear of dirty dishes.

FRUIT FLIES

Having fruit flies circling around the basket of bananas on your kitchen counter makes you shudder a little, right? If you've never seen one up close, they're small, tan flies. They like to eat ripe or rotting produce, and they're drawn to dampness. You really don't want them around because they carry bacteria on their legs and reproduce very quickly. So how do you make sure they're not interested in your kitchen? Your overall goal should be to minimize the smells of ripe produce and any dampness that might attract fruit flies. Here are our best tips:

- Keep produce in a container or in the refrigerator
- Empty your trash cans regularly
- Clean your kitchen sink and drain
- Keep an eye out for spills and clean them up properly

If you do end up with fruit flies around, we also have a few tips on how to get rid of them. Here are some low-key home remedies for fruit flies:

- **Vinegar traps.** Either white vinegar and apple cider vinegar will work in this simple trap. Fill a small bowl with vinegar and add a few drops of dish soap on top. The vinegar will draw the fruit flies in, and the dish soap will break the surface tension enough that the flies will fall straight through and drown. You can clean them up easily that way.
- **Overripe fruit.** Take a piece of fruit past its prime and place it in an open plastic baggie. The flies will enter the baggie to eat the fruit, and then you can seal it up and toss them.
- **Chemical sprays.** You can always use an insecticide to get rid of fruit flies, too. This method can usually only be used to kill fruit flies one after the other or in small groups, so it shouldn't be used as an overall treatment, but if you spot a fruit fly errantly buzzing around, a good spritz of insecticide will do the trick.

BEDBUGS

Everyone dreads finding out that they have bedbugs. In fact, some lease agreements even have a "bedbug addendum," which outlines the steps renters must take in order to prevent bedbug infestations. Bedbugs are found most often in bed parts, like mattresses and box springs; however, all kinds of crevices appeal to them. People often end up carrying them from place to place in their luggage. How do you know if they're living in your bed? You'll wake up with red, itchy welts from their bites, often seen in a straight line on your skin. You might also spot the bugs themselves: they're reddish-brown and flat, like apple seeds (only smaller). While the good news is that bedbugs don't carry any disease, we're sure you'll still want to get rid of them. To prevent them in the first place, here are our tips:

- Clean up your clutter
- Check your clothes, suitcases, and mattresses while traveling and upon return
- Patch up crevices and cracks near your bed

If you do end up spotting bedbugs, you'll definitely want to call an extermination company. (This will probably involve coordinating with your landlord, so make sure you get in touch with them first.) With some of the other pests we discuss, you might be able to control the problem yourself, but this isn't really the case with bedbugs because only an extermination company will be able to ensure the bugs are dead. Likely, they will heat your room or your whole apartment to the right temperature to kill the bugs. While you wait for an exterminator, though, here are a couple of other tips:

- **Clean up all the visible bugs.** Before the professionals arrive, it will help if you clean the affected areas. This means vacuuming the spaces with visible bed bugs and washing and drying your bedding on the highest heat setting. The heat will help to kill the bugs.

- **Use a mattress protector.** In order to contain the problem, you can seal your mattress in a zip-up mattress protector. The bugs won't be able to get in or out of the plastic. This won't kill the bed bugs, as they can go a year without food(!), but it will at least prevent more of them from getting into your mattress. You can also use a mattress protector from the beginning as a preventative measure to stop bedbugs from getting in at all.

ANTS

As far as pests go, ants are definitely one of the more harmless kinds. They don't carry disease, and they don't usually do much damage, but they can be an incredible nuisance. If you want to prevent them from getting into your apartment, here are our best tips:

- Seal cracks and crevices in walls and floors—and inspect regularly to make sure no new ones have appeared
- Keep food containers tightly closed and avoid leaving crumbs and other messes on countertops
- Keep your eyes peeled for "scout ants" looking for food and water sources

If ants do end up invading your home, there are lots of different ways to get rid of them. The obvious one that jumps to mind is insecticide. That will only kill a few ants, though, and if you have pets, you'll want to be super cautious that they don't end up eating any of the poison. If you can, you want to find out where the ants' colony is and target that instead. We understand that this might not be possible in an apartment building, however. We're going to offer two solutions that will target the ants' colony and two nontoxic ant deterrents.

- **Ant bait.** You can buy slow-acting pesticide to poison the ants' food source in their colony. The pesticides come disguised in sweet, fatty bait, and the ants will take this bait back to their food stores. Then, the pesticides will kill all of the ants that eat it. This will kill many more ants than spraying them with an insecticide would.

- **Boiling water.** This is an easy and effective way to kill ants if you've located their colony outside. Simply pour a kettle of boiling water over the colony, and it should kill off most, if not all, of them.
- **Vinegar.** Undiluted vinegar will kill ants if they are sprayed with it, so by keeping some vinegar around in a spray bottle, you can get rid of ants as you see them in your apartment.
- **Spices and oils.** Ants hate strong smells, so kitchen spices (like cinnamon and cumin powder) and essential oils (like tea tree and peppermint) will act as deterrents. You can sprinkle them around your doorways to ward off ants. You'll just want to be careful that pets and small children do not ingest these.

COCKROACHES

Ah, cockroaches—you've probably heard tons about them, and chances are you've seen your fair share of them. Cockroaches carry bacteria, and they'll contaminate any food product they touch. They also leave an unpleasant odor throughout your apartment. Unfortunately, they can be quite difficult to get rid of, but prevention is easier. To stop them from getting into your apartment, here are our best tips:

- Inspect groceries and boxes from storage when you bring them into your home
- Dine in one area and avoid eating outside of that area to avoid spreading crumbs throughout your apartment
- Caulk small holes and gaps in your floors, walls, windows, and doorways to prevent roaches from entering
- Wash dishes promptly and don't leave dirty dishes or water in the sink
- Don't store cardboard boxes (cockroaches eat the glue that holds boxes together)

- Report any leaks in your place that you notice, since wherever there is water, cockroaches like to make a home

If you do end up seeing cockroaches around your apartment, you should call an extermination company as soon as you can. One cockroach usually means there are more around, and the situation can get out of hand very quickly. While you wait for the exterminator, here are a few strategies to help you get your roaches under control:

- **Baking soda.** This is an easy, cost-effective way to get rid of roaches, and you probably have some baking soda in your cupboard. By mixing baking soda with sugar, onions, or another type of roach-friendly food, you'll have cockroach bait. Once the roaches eat the food, the baking soda will create gasses in their stomachs that will make them explode. Gross but effective.
- **Bait stations.** You can buy bait stations prepped with poisonous cockroach bait. Once the cockroaches eat the poison, they will bring it back to their home and pass it on to the other cockroaches. This will ensure that more than just a few of them die. Of course, you'll want to ensure that you keep the poisonous bait and the poisoned dead cockroaches away from any pets and children and, if possible, any other animals that might ingest them.
- **Glue traps.** Glue traps are sticky strips that you can place where you commonly see cockroaches. The cockroaches will get stuck on these traps once they walk over them. The traps won't kill the roaches, so you'll have to find a way to dispose of them yourself. You'll also want to make sure that you and your other housemates don't walk over any of the traps yourselves.

FLEAS

If you have pets, then you're probably already concerned about fleas. Even if you don't have pets, fleas can still find their way into your apartment.

Unlike most pests listed here, fleas eat blood rather than discarded food. This means that they are considered external parasites. So how do you make sure they don't find their way into your rental apartment?

- If you have pets, limit the time they spend outdoors and inspect them regularly for fleas
- After you spend time outdoors, make sure to inspect skin and articles of clothing for fleas
- Clean and vacuum all areas of your apartment regularly

Let's say fleas do get into your apartment, through your pet or otherwise. What do you do now? Fleas can be really tough to fight back against, but there are a few things you can do to try to get your flea issue under control. We've tried to suggest nontoxic, less-invasive ways to get rid of fleas rather than chemical solutions such as flea bombs.

- **Vacuum every day.** Yes, every day, vacuum all of your surfaces. Your vacuum is actually one of the most effective flea killers in your home. Fleas are attracted to vacuums because of their vibrations, so it's easy to capture them this way. The turbulence of being tossed around in the vacuum's trap will kill them. Therefore, you want to make sure that you're vacuuming every possible surface in your home. Use a hose attachment to make sure you get in all the nooks and crannies.
- **Wash human and animal bedding.** Fleas like to hide away in bedding, so it's important to make sure that you wash your own bedding and your pet's (if you have a pet). Wash it on high heat and, if you can, machine-dry it—the heat and vibrations will help to kill the fleas.
- **Use a nontoxic spray.** Look for a nontoxic flea spray and use it to spray down all of the carpeted and upholstered surfaces in your home. Most sprays like this will kill fleas within seconds of touching them. This will ensure that you kill as many fleas as possible even if your vacuum doesn't catch them.

BEES

Bees are great for your local ecosystem, but we know that it can be unpleasant to have them in or around your apartment. This is especially true if you're allergic to bee stings. We've found a few of the best ways to prevent bees from coming into your apartment, so use these if you notice bees near your building.

- Repair holes in window screens
- Be mindful of what flowers you plant if you have a balcony—bees are attracted to bright colors and certain types of plants
- Avoid keeping unused objects such as buckets, pipes, and hoses on your balcony, as bees might want to nest in them

If you do get bees in your apartment, we know you'll want them out as soon as possible. However, you'll want to be careful to get the bees to leave without hurting them. Bees are very important to the environment, and their populations are declining rapidly. It's best to try to get them to leave without hurting them, so none of the suggestions below involve killing or harming the bees.

- **Crushed garlic.** Bees hate the smell of garlic. Leaving crushed garlic around your place is the most effective method, but sprinkling garlic powder works, too.
- **Cinnamon.** Bees also hate cinnamon. Leave a few sticks of cinnamon around your windowsills to drive bees away. You can sprinkle ground cinnamon, too.
- **Beekeepers.** If you have a pervasive bee problem, it's best to call a beekeeper. These professionals can locate the hive and remove it safely without harming the bees. The bees won't bother you anymore, and they'll still be able to do their jobs as pollinators. You might even get a bunch of jars of honey when they're done. Wins all around!

Most of these tips will work to keep wasps away, too. However, you don't want to call a beekeeper if you have a wasp issue; instead, you'll want to call an extermination company. Remember to talk to your landlord first before you reach out to an exterminator.

MOTHS

Seeing a cluster of moths around a porch light is one of summer's most common sights. When they're in your apartment, however, they're a little more alarming. At first, you might mistake moths for butterflies, but their dusky gray color and feathery antennae will tip you off. There are a few easy ways to make sure that your apartment isn't super moth friendly:

- Moths are attracted to lights, so turn off lights when you're not using them
- Moths nest in old clothes and stored grains, so make sure to check your closets and pantry regularly for moth eggs; seal everything in airtight containers and vacuum bags
- Vacuum your closet and pantry regularly to catch moth eggs

So, what if you start seeing moths everywhere in your apartment? There are a few key signs that you could have a more serious moth problem on your hands, like holes and larvae in your clothes and cocoons in your cupboards. Here are a few ways you can get rid of the moths in your home:

- **Freeze your clothes.** Freezing your infested clothes before washing them will help you kill all of the moth larvae. Make sure that you leave them in your freezer for at least seventy-two hours once they reach freezing temperature.
- **Vinegar and water solutions.** The acid in vinegar will kill moths, so you can make a spray of equal parts vinegar and water to treat any areas where you spot the critters. You can also wipe down

different parts of your home with this solution to discourage the moths from coming near.

- **Moth traps.** Pheromone moth traps are made up of glue and cardboard. They attract male moths by using female moths' pheromones, and when the moths fly into the traps, they stick to the glue and die soon after.

SPIDERS

The sight of a spider is enough to send chills down many people's spines. You can recognize them by their eight legs and distinctive webs. There are hundreds of spider species, but in houses and apartments, common house spiders are the ones you're most likely to spot. We have a few suggestions to help prevent spiders from getting into your apartment:

- Seal any cracks and gaps in the walls—spiders can get into even the smallest ones
- Declutter and clean as much as possible, both inside your apartment and the areas around the exterior of the building
- Use essential oils and citrus as natural spider repellents

If you do end up with a spider problem, there will be a few key signs. You'll notice their webs in corners of your apartment and on door frames, and you might see egg sacs, too. With certain types of spiders, you'll also get a few spider bites on your skin. These are red, inflamed, and itchy, and sometimes they have two holes where the spider's fangs punctured your skin. So how do you get rid of spiders once they're in your apartment?

- **Vacuum.** When you see webs or egg sacs around your apartment, suck them up with your vacuum cleaner. This will stop the spiders from reproducing, an absolute necessity for stopping an infestation.
- **Vinegar and water.** Yes, vinegar works for spiders, too! A solution of equal parts vinegar and water will kill spiders if you spray

them. This approach is easy and nontoxic—what more could you want?

- **Glue traps.** When spiders run across these sticky traps, they get stuck on the glue and then die. These work best when you have a bunch of spiders rather than just one or two. Set them around the places where you most commonly see spiders, and you'll be sure to snag them.

RODENTS

Mice, rats, and other rodents are some of the least welcome critters you can find in your apartment. You can generally employ the same methods to get rid of them, regardless of the species. And there are a few things you can do to prevent rodents from getting into your apartment to begin with:

- Make sure to keep your kitchen free from crumbs and spills, and make sure that your food is sealed tightly in hard plastic containers
- Seal up any holes in the walls and floors of your apartment (inside and out) with a combination of steel wool and caulk to ensure that rodents cannot chew new holes in the same place
- Keep your trash can covered

If you do end up with a rodent infestation, you'll see a few signs: chew marks on your food's packaging, droppings around your apartment, scratching sounds in the walls, and maybe even the little guys themselves scurrying across the floor. So what can you do to get rid of them?

- **Traps.** There are tons of different traps to choose from, ranging from classic wooden snap traps to glue traps. Some will keep the rodent alive, some will kill it on contact, some involve bait, and some don't. You can choose a trap style that suits you best.

- **Pets.** Your cat, and even sometimes your dog, can help to keep your apartment's rodent population under control. Their natural hunting instincts will help them kill rodents without any help or direction from you. Plus, your pet will provide a constant threat that might make rodents less eager to enter your apartment to begin with.
- **Ultrasonic repellent.** Ultrasonic repellents have an immediate effect on rodent populations, but they don't work over time. However, you can use this type of repellent as a short-term solution while you call an exterminator, set traps, or both, depending on the size of your infestation.

As is the case for all of the pests we mention, you will almost certainly need professional help for a rodent infestation. Getting rid of rodents takes specialized skill, so be sure that you call a professional before your rodent problem becomes too much to handle.

SQUIRRELS

You'd normally expect to see squirrels outside of your apartment, but they can occasionally make their homes on rooftops or find their way into your walls. Signs of a squirrel infestation include scratching and tearing noises within your walls, rips on garbage bags by the curb of your building, squirrel droppings, and squirrel footprints. There are a few things you can do to ensure that squirrels stay away from your apartment.

- Avoid having bird feeders on your balcony, as these attract squirrels
- Trim back tree branches over your balcony (ask your landlord first)
- Keep your window screens in good repair

Unfortunately, if you do end up with squirrels in your walls, there isn't a DIY way to get rid of the infestation. They might go away on their own, but it's unlikely. You should let your landlord know, and they will call pest control.

BIRDS

As with squirrels, you won't normally have to deal with birds inside of your apartment. Sometimes, however, birds can nest in apartment-building vents. The smell of their droppings and their excessive chirping might bother you.

There's not a lot you can do to avoid this issue in your own unit, but you can tell your landlord. They'll fix the issue by hiring a company to remove the nest or by getting rid of it themself if it is inactive. If the bird species happens to be a protected one, you and your landlord will have to wait until the chicks have flown away in order to be able to legally remove the nest. This could take a few weeks.

MOLD

The last thing you want to see crawling up your bathroom wall is a patch of mold. Fuzzy, discolored, and totally gross, mold tends to pop up when you least expect it. Most often, you'll find it on damp, porous surfaces, like wood. But if you take a few preventative measures, you might never have to deal with any mold growth in your apartment.

- **Check regularly on the most mold-friendly spots.** Think about the places in your rental where mold is most likely to grow. Dark, damp corners and leaky spots are good places to start. You'll want to be particularly careful in your bathroom and kitchen because there's running water in both of those places. Do what you can to keep them dry, and check them regularly to see if mold is growing.
- **Be aware of how your habits might create mold.** Do you leave your wet towel on your wood floor after a shower? Do you

forget to run your bathroom fan when you shower? Do you let your clothes sit in the washer for a while before moving them to the dryer? These habits encourage mold. If you change small moisture-spreading habits such as these, you can stop mold growth in its tracks.

- **Watch out for your plants.** Yup, your beautiful plants can bring mold into your apartment. Their damp soil is ideal for mold. A quick tip: make sure you only water your plants when they're dry. This will prevent mold growth, and on top of that, it's healthier for your plants, too.
- **Invest in mold-prevention products.** Keep a few mold-prevention products on hand. There are tons out there for you to choose from—removers, cleaners, sprays, all kinds of fun things. Without these, make sure you have some white vinegar on hand because it kills lots of different types of mold.

What to Do If You Discover Mold

So what do you do if you find mold in your apartment? First, spray it down with some white vinegar. Then, let your landlord know. The two of you will work together to determine the source of the problem and find a solution. If it's something bigger, like a leaky pipe, your landlord will fix it. However, if the mold growth is because of your own habits, you'll likely have to fix the issue yourself. Long showers and towels on the floor are common habits that would lead to you being on the hook for mold removal.

Hopefully you never actually have to deal with mold in your rental. Prevention is best in this case, so use our list of tips, and you should be just fine.

Remember: Call your landlord or the exterminator as soon as things get out of hand—or before, if possible. Creepy-crawlies can get out of control very quickly.

4.12

HELP! MY LANDLORD IS SELLING MY PLACE. WHAT DO I DO?

One of the biggest surprises you can face as a renter is hearing that your landlord is selling your home. What does the sale mean for you?

From the perspective of a renter, there's two parts to the sale process. The first is the marketing of the property, and the second is the actual transition to a new owner. Let's tackle those separately.

PART 1: YOUR HOME IS BEING MARKETED

If you live in a big property, like a 100+ unit apartment community, you may not even notice that there's a sale happening. You may notice a couple of extra folks visiting the property, and then maybe some new people in the office, but these types of transactions are really financial ones, and there's not that much that should bother or affect you.

If you're in a small property—a single-family rental or a three-unit building, for example—then the sale process almost always sucks for you, the renter and the occupant of the property that's being sold.

To manage this process, it helps to know what your rights are and what the landlord's rights are. Some specific questions to look for in your lease:

- How much notice does the landlord have to give you for a showing?
- Is there a limit to the number of times the landlord can access your home during a set period of time?
- Are there any specific rules pertaining to a sale/marketing process?
- How far in advance does your landlord have to inform you that you will need to vacate the property, according to your area's laws?

Most of the frustration and friction that we've seen with sale processes come down to either the landlord or the resident not being familiar with the rules. Make sure you understand the rules as laid out by your lease, and confirm that your landlord knows them as well.

Can You Turn the Marketing of Your Home to Your Advantage?

In most normal sale situations, there's nothing in it for you, but you do have to deal with your landlord being stressed about whether your home is clean and tidy, sending extra maintenance folks over (which you may or may not think is necessary), and prospective buyers traipsing through your home, often with minimal notice. None of this is pleasant.

It does, however, make a difference to your landlord that these things go smoothly. If your place is a mess and you're making it difficult for the landlord to show your place to prospective buyers, that's going to cost your landlord real money because buyers will feel like the property isn't as well maintained as it might otherwise be, and some buyers who might have been interested may never be able to see the property.

That said, there is a potential opportunity here for you. Because the landlord is about to get a payday, make it worth your while to support them. One strategy is to request some sort of win-win situation to make you feel better about all of this.

You could, for example, ask for a discount on rent while the marketing is going on or for a rebate upon the successful sale of the property. If you really want to get aggressive, the landlord may be interested in promising "vacant possession" (that's when you move out) to the new owner, and you could ask for compensation in return for moving out early.

Whatever you agree upon, make sure you get it in writing, and if you're owed money upon a successful sale, make sure it's settled at the closing table when all the money changes hands between the buyer and seller. It can be very difficult to chase down a landlord who's already sold your property and try to make a claim at that point.

And, of course, if you negotiate a deal like this, then make sure you keep up your end of the deal.

PART 2: SALE OF YOUR SINGLE-FAMILY HOME OR TOWNHOME

What happens after the sale of the property mostly comes down to the nature of the buyer who has purchased from your landlord and the plans they have for your place.

Is the buyer planning to be a landlord? Or are they planning to use the property as their residence? Is the buyer going to keep the place as is? Or do they want to make lots of improvements to the property with the intention of getting a lot more rent from each unit?

The best way to find out your new landlord's plans is to ask them. Usually, there will be an opportunity to speak to them shortly after the purchase.

Note that it's pretty rare to speak to a new landlord before the purchase is completed. Usually, the new and old landlords are both focused on getting the deal done, and many of these types of deals fall apart at some point along the path to a sale. As a result, the old landlord is usually pretty protective of the existing renters because they want as little disruption for you as possible and the new landlord doesn't know if the deal is closed for sure, so they'll wait until everything's finalized to chat with you directly.

Depending on what your interests are with the property and whether you want to stay there, the best scenario for you is usually the landlord who comes in and wants to maintain the property as is. Unfortunately, this isn't the most common scenario.

Usually, when a new landlord purchases a place, they have some sort of plan in mind for making more money from the property than the prior owners made. Or they have a different use for the property in mind—for example, they might want to live in it themselves.

Regardless, the most important thing for you at this point is to know your lease and therefore your rights.

- When does your lease expire?
- Do you have a right to renew at lease expiration?
- Are there any parts of your lease that specifically address what happens when a new owner takes possession?

Reviewing these lease terms will help you know what your rights are so that you can work with your new landlord in full possession of your rights. And, if there's a change coming, it helps ensure that you can plan appropriately.

Can the New Owner Move You Out?

In general, no, the new owner cannot make you move out. The new owner has purchased the building or apartment, and that means they have to take over the lease, and your rights in the lease continue regardless of the new owner.

But here's the bad news. In most parts of the United States, the landlord doesn't have to offer you a renewal. So, when your lease ends, they can refuse to renew your lease, meaning that then, you will have to move out and find another place. For that reason, you'll want to be sure that you seek out some other rental opportunities when the end of your lease is in view.

There are some places across the country and some types of properties where you may have the right to renew automatically. These are rare, but they do exist, most often in cities in the Northeastern United States or on the West Coast.

To find out if you may have rights like this, talk to your local renters' rights organization. We have an ever-growing list of those organizations at Dwellsy.com/blog/rentersorganizations.

SIGNS THAT YOUR LANDLORD IS SELLING YOUR RENTAL

Ideally, your landlord will be straightforward with you if they're going to sell your rental unit. In a perfect world, they'd warn you well in advance and keep you in the loop the whole time. This doesn't always happen, though. Here are a few common warning signs that your landlord may be selling your rental or the whole building.

- **People coming in and out of your place.** Is there a stream of new folks coming in and out of your apartment and your building? Maybe some are people viewing the building or the unit. Others may be architects or people coming by to measure everything. This is a pretty good sign your landlord is thinking about selling.
- **Sudden improvements.** Surprise! Your landlord wants to rip out that nasty old carpet and put in a brand-new one. They're updating the lighting fixtures, too, and giving you an upgraded fridge. This is another sign that your landlord is thinking about selling: they want to make the place look great so that they can ask for a higher price.
- **Rumors are flying.** Of course, you can't believe everything everyone says. If some of your neighbors have also heard that the landlord is selling, it may or may not be true. It's still worth talking to them to find out what they know and compare notes, however; maybe one of them saw something you didn't, like a stream of executives that came to look the place over while you were at work.

Remember that these are all just signs and that nothing is certain until your landlord says so. Even if you see all of the warning signs above, it may just be a coincidence, so try not to jump to conclusions. If you're starting to think your landlord might sell, the best thing to do is ask them. Maybe you'll learn that something completely different is going on and that nothing will impact your lease. If your landlord says that they are going to sell, or even if they're evasive and unclear in their answer, that's a good sign that you may want to be ready for the marketing process and for an eventual sale.

Remember: Tackle a potential sale of your home directly with your landlord to make sure you don't get surprised and to potentially even find a way to benefit.

4.13

WHAT TO DO WHEN SOMETHING GOES WRONG (EVICTIONS)

Obviously, the last thing you want is to be evicted from your rental. We're sure you're determined to do everything in your power to ensure that you're never at risk of eviction. It would impact not only your credit for years but also your ability to rent at another place once it's on your record. Emergencies and other unexpected issues can happen to anyone, though, so it's always good to be prepared.

When you imagine being evicted, your mind is probably enveloped by fear and panic. We understand why you'd have this reaction—most people would. That's part of why we want to talk about it now. The better you understand what happens during an eviction, the less panicked you'll be if you ever find yourself facing one. So let's talk it through and try to break down evictions, one step at a time.

One more thing before we get started: it's important to note that eviction procedures can vary quite a bit depending on what state you live in. We'll describe the general outline of how evictions occur, but make sure to check your state laws to more fully understand how things will go.

WHY YOUR TENANCY MIGHT BE TERMINATED

First, let's discuss why your landlord might end your tenancy. This is a good thing to understand even if you're not at risk of it happening so that you can understand how best to avoid it. Your landlord might end your tenancy if you are:

- not paying your rent
- violating your lease in some way
- damaging or refusing to care for the rental
- engaging in illegal activity on the rental property, such as vandalism or drug dealing
- engaging in activity that can cause harm to other residents

Any one of these activities puts you at risk of lease termination, especially if there are repeated incidents or if you do more than one of them.

TERMINATION NOTICES VS. EVICTIONS

If your landlord wants to end your tenancy, the first step they will generally take is sending you a termination notice. A termination notice tells you that your lease is ending or that it will end if you don't pay your rent or fix a certain problem within the given time frame. This is not an eviction.

An eviction is the process of filing a lawsuit and going to court against a tenant if they don't leave the rental property within the termination-notice period. If a landlord gives a tenant a termination notice, and then they move out within the stated period of time, they will not have been evicted. You cannot be evicted without a court order.

In most states, landlords are required to send tenants a termination notice in order to begin the eviction process, so you will be informed ahead of time if you are anywhere close to being evicted. There may be other signs before this stage—perhaps you'll receive written or verbal warnings—but a termination notice is where the landlord begins to fulfill their legal obligations. They are not required to give you any indication that they are going to send you a termination notice, so the notice might be the first indication of any potential eviction that you see.

If you receive a termination notice, don't panic. This is your landlord's way of letting you know that your tenancy is in danger, so it's also your chance to figure out a solution. It's a legal requirement as a first step in an eviction process in many cases, so there are a lot more termination notices or three-day notices out there than you might suspect.

Our goal in this section is to make sure that you never face an eviction lawsuit, so most of our discussion will be centered around understanding lease terminations and how to deal with them before you are ever officially evicted. However, we will also talk a little bit about eviction lawsuits and what happens during them.

UNDERSTANDING DIFFERENT KINDS OF LEASE TERMINATIONS

There are a few different kinds of lease terminations you could receive, so let's review them.

Most lease terminations fall under the category of "notice of termination for cause." This means that the landlord will give you a reason why your lease is being terminated. In most cases, you'll have a chance to fix the situation before you're evicted. Here are the types of notices you might receive in this case:

- **Pay rent or quit.** This is the type of notice you'll receive if you haven't been paying your rent on time. It will list the amount you owe—your unpaid rent plus fees—and tell you within how many days you must pay before you are officially evicted. (This amount of time will vary by state, but it's usually anywhere from three to five days.) It's important to note that with this kind of notice, you can't just move out, because your landlord can still sue you for unpaid rent.
- **Cure or quit.** This is the type of notice you'll receive if you've been violating your lease or not taking care of your rental. Like

the "pay rent or quit" notice, you'll have a few days to "cure" the lease violation (and the exact amount of time still depends on the state). Unlike "pay rent or quit" notices, however, you can simply move out if you receive a "cure or quit" notice.

- **Unconditional quit.** Your landlord will serve you an "unconditional quit" notice if they are not offering you a way to remedy the situation and are simply letting you know that your lease is terminated. Most states will only let a landlord serve this type of notice in specific circumstances. If you have violated your lease multiple times or severely damaged your property, for example, you might be given this type of notice. The amount of time that a landlord has to give you to move out after an "unconditional quit" notice will vary by state, too, so check your local laws.
- **Notice of termination without cause.** This applies if your lease is month-to-month. These notices mean that your landlord is asking you to move out even though you haven't done anything wrong. Even if you pay your bills on time, stick to the rules of the lease, and do everything else you're supposed to, your landlord can still ask you to leave at any time as long as they give you enough notice. This notice period will vary depending on the state, but it's usually around thirty days.

YOUR LANDLORD CAN'T THREATEN TO EVICT YOU

It's important to remember that your landlord is not allowed to threaten you with eviction or harass you into leaving the rental property. If you violate your lease, however, your landlord can ask you to correct the violation and remind you that you could be evicted if the violation continues. (These are the kinds of warning signs that might hint at an upcoming termination notice, as we mentioned earlier.)

WHAT TO DO IF YOU RECEIVE A TERMINATION NOTICE

If you receive a termination notice, the first thing to do is not to panic. Keeping a cool head will be a great help in this situation because you'll need to do quite a bit of thinking and weighing of your options. And you do have options, even though you may feel trapped and desperate. We know you don't want to be evicted. Let's walk through your next steps.

Don't Leave Your Home Right Away

As we've already discussed, in pretty much every case, you'll have a few days to remedy whatever has gone wrong. There's no need to start frantically packing boxes when you're not even sure if you'll have to move and before you have a place to go. Instead, think about how you might potentially fix the problem. You might not have to move at all.

Know Your Rights

Understanding your rights is important in this case. You have the right to a termination notice and a certain notice period. Make sure that you receive all the time and information you are legally entitled to depending on where you live.

Remember that you have a legal right not to be harassed by your landlord. Commonly, landlords threaten tenants with eviction, and, as you know, this is illegal. Other forms of harassment include:

- Changing or threatening to change the locks
- Moving your belongings
- Pressuring you to move before you legally have to
- Shutting off utilities
- Violent or intimidating actions, language, or behavior

If you feel that you are being harassed, speak to a landlord–tenant attorney or get another form of legal aid as soon as possible.

Read Your Lease

Read your lease and your state and local laws to find out exactly what they say about how eviction is handled. It's possible that the notice you were served violates the terms of the lease or even that the lease violates the law. If your termination notice claims that you violated the lease, rereading the lease will also help you understand what you need to do in order to obey the lease exactly.

Talk to Your Landlord

Set up a meeting with your landlord as soon as possible. If you've received a "pay rent or quit" or a "cure or quit" notice, you want to make sure that they know you intend to fix the issue. Talking things out will communicate to them that you understand the extent of the problem, and it will also help you understand what you need to do to get things back on track.

Even if you've received an unconditional notice or a notice without cause, you can still talk to your landlord and try to work something out. There's a chance that you can come to an agreement that doesn't end in you moving.

As always, both you and your landlord should behave professionally and politely at all times. Keep your rights in mind and advocate for yourself. Take notes during the meeting, both for your own memory and in case you eventually need evidence in court.

Understand the Timeline

Remember that there will be a certain amount of time between a termination notice and an eviction lawsuit. Check exactly what your state's laws say about how long you should have, and make sure that all communications from your landlord reinforce that expectation. As you either remedy your current rental situation or look for a new place to live, you'll want to be aware of where you are in that timeline so that you understand the next steps.

Research and Apply for Legal and Financial Aid

If you feel that you're in serious danger of eviction, do some research on renters' aid organizations in your state. They may be able to help you pay your rent or provide legal assistance if you have to go to court.

The US Department of the Treasury disburses emergency rental assistance (ERA) through state and local programs. Through their funds, they can help you cover rent, utilities, and home energy costs. Through the Department of the Treasury's website, you can find local programs and determine if you're eligible for their assistance.

You can also reach out to mutual-aid networks in your area to find out if they may be able to help you.

Through resources such as the American Bar Association's legal-help finder, the National Fair Housing Alliance's website, and HUD's list of approved housing-counseling services, you may be able to find low- or no-cost legal aid.

Find a New Place

If you do need to find a new place to live, it might be possible for you to move in with your parents, other family, or a friend. Think about who in your life might have extra space for you while you look for a new living situation. Don't be afraid to ask for help.

If you need to find a rental fast, refer back to Section 3.5. You could secure a new rental within days.

WHAT HAPPENS IF YOUR LANDLORD FILES AN EVICTION LAWSUIT

If the period of notice in your lease termination goes by and you haven't fixed the problem or moved out, your landlord will likely file an eviction lawsuit against you.

Before the eviction trial, research the specific processes for your city or state, as they can vary quite widely. Regardless, you will need to prepare evidence to defend your position. Remember to bring three copies—one for you, one for the court, and one for the landlord.

It is important that you appear on the court date set for your trial because the judge will likely decide against you if you don't show up, no matter how convincing your case is.

We recommend doing everything possible to avoid getting to this point because if you go to court and the court evicts you, it will appear on your record and could make it much harder for you to get housing. The eviction will be removed from your record after seven years.

If you do end up with an eviction on your record, it will make it harder for you to rent in the future, but it won't be impossible. Treat the situation as if you had bad credit or something else that made you a less-than-ideal tenant, and work on the other aspects of your renter profile. You can:

- Sit down and talk to potential landlords about your eviction so that they hear the full story
- Try to rent through owners and not through companies, since individual landlords may be more lenient
- Get a cosigner
- Offer a bigger security deposit, higher rent, or more rent up front
- Work to improve your credit score
- Make sure your references are solid

These aren't your only options. Sometimes, if you settle your debts and speak to your old landlord, they may be willing to remove the eviction from your tenant-screening report. This depends on your landlord, however, so you're better off trying to avoid being evicted in the first place.

Hopefully you understand lease terminations and evictions better than you did at the beginning of this section. We know that even thinking about evictions can be scary, never mind facing one. Remember, this process is not an immediate one. These things take time. There are resources and help available to you as a renter if you're at risk of eviction.

Remember: Evictions can stick with you for years. Don't be afraid to stand up for your rights, but at all costs, try to avoid an actual eviction process.

Section 5

RENEWING AND MOVING ON

The end of your lease is approaching and it's time to start thinking about what comes next for you. Or maybe it's not the end of your lease, but you find yourself needing to think about what's next and if the same or a different living situation suits you. This section is for you.

In this section, we'll cover how to:

- Renew your lease
- Move out and get as much of your security deposit back as possible
- Handle moving out before the end of your lease

5.1

120 DAYS BEFORE THE END OF YOUR LEASE

Remember that day, forever ago, when you moved into your new place? Time flies, and too many of us are surprised when the end of our lease approaches. For many of our friends, they're reminded of the end of the lease by the landlord reaching out to ask if they'll be renewing or not.

Don't be that renter. Because if you are, you've already given up a couple of big advantages in the renewal and move-out processes.

Because you need a place to live 365 days a year and your lease has a fixed timeline, time is of the essence if you want to have control over your living situation. The more you can control the timeline, the better chance you have of living in the place you want rather than settling for less.

So, first off, know when 120 days before your lease end is, and mark that in your calendar when you sign the lease so you can be ready later.

When you get to that 120-day point, there are a couple of things to do.

CHECK YOUR LEASE

You're looking for a few things in that lease that you may not recall from when you read it in the beginning.

First, you're looking for the lease end date, just to confirm it's when you think it is. You're also looking to confirm whether or not the lease end date has a time attached to it. Some leases say you have to be out by a particular time of day, and some just have a day, which generally means you need to be out by close of business.

Second, you're looking for how much advance notice you need to give if you are moving out. One of the reasons we're suggesting you start this process 120 days in advance is that you might have to give notice as many as ninety days in advance. More often, it's thirty, forty-five, or sixty days.

It's also important to check exactly how to give your notice. Some landlords want an actual paper letter with an ink signature, while others are happy with an email, text, or phone call or for you to stop by the office. Reading your lease should let you know exactly what you need to do. But, remember, this notice is the kind of thing you will likely want to document, so it's usually best to send it in a way that is time-stamped and where there is a record that you can keep (like an email).

Third, make sure you understand what happens if you choose to stay in the place. In some leases, you can automatically roll over to a new annual lease or a month-to-month lease, sometimes without a rent increase and sometimes with a predetermined rent increase. Understanding where you stand can help you evaluate your options.

Fourth, start thinking about what comes next for you. Did you like living in your place? Does it still work for you? If so, then perhaps you want to explore renewing your lease and staying. If not, then you might want to consider how you can find a place that works better for you.

Fifth, take a look around the market. See what's available and how it compares to your place. Hopping on Dwellsy and both taking a look at places like yours and thinking about other types of places that might be even better for you will help you understand where the market prices are and how your other options compare with your current place.

Some years ago, Jonas had a renewal coming up on the apartment he was living in and did exactly this. He was shocked to find out that similar apartments nearby were now priced at about 10–15 percent *less* than what he was paying.

Sixty days in advance of his lease renewal and before his landlord could reach out with a renewal offer (and anchor on a rent price—remember that concept from the negotiation section?), he reached out to the landlord and requested a renewal with a 10 percent rent reduction for the coming year.

His landlord was shocked but did her own research and ultimately came to the conclusion that he was right and that his requested rent was a reasonable market rate for the apartment at that time. Not what she would have asked for if she'd been the one to reach out first, that's for sure!

WHAT IF I CAN'T DECIDE WHETHER TO RENEW MY LEASE OR MOVE OUT?

Maybe you're not sure whether you want to renew your lease or move out. It can be a tough decision to make, with plenty of factors to weigh. There are a few key questions you can ask yourself when you're thinking things through:

- **Do you like your rental?** This one is obvious, but sometimes, the answer is not quite as clear as you'd think. Often, in our day-to-day lives, we make all kinds of little adjustments to certain inconveniences, and then we forget that we're being inconvenienced. For example, maybe the water in your building takes ten minutes to heat after you've turned on the shower and you've lived with that. Maybe there are frequent blackouts and you've put up with them. Take stock of these things when you're thinking about whether you want to keep living in your apartment. It could be the case that you really do like your current place, and that's great.

- **Do you like your neighborhood?** This is another good thing to consider. Maybe you'd like more restaurants or green spaces. Maybe it's hard to find an open grocery store at the time you usually like to shop and you want more options. Maybe you just don't feel safe where you live. This is a good opportunity to switch neighborhoods if you'd like to. If you love the area but not your apartment, you can always stay in the neighborhood and just find another rental nearby.
- **Do you like your landlord?** Yep, you should think about this. If your landlord is awful at communicating with you or has treated you unkindly, it's worth thinking seriously about moving out. After all, the situation might become worse over time. On the other hand, if you have a great relationship with your landlord, maybe that's a reason to stay.
- **Can you still afford your rental's rate?** Your landlord might raise your rent when you renew, particularly if you initially got a deal or if the price of your rental was comparatively low when you moved in. Do some research and find out how similar rentals are priced in your area. Maybe you'll find out that you're actually paying above the market rate and you can negotiate lower rent this time around.
- **Can you afford to move out?** Moving can be expensive. It involves everything from security deposits to movers' fees to the price of packing materials. You'll also spend a lot of time and energy getting everything done. You might have to take time off work or cancel other commitments. Make sure you can afford to move before you decide not to renew your lease.
- **How's the rental market?** Is the rent skyrocketing where you are, or are prices unusually low? Do some research and find out. That way, you can make the smartest financial decision. Remember, there are certain times of year when it's better to search for rentals—check out Section 1.8 for more details on that.

These questions are only a starting point. Only you can weigh things out for yourself and make the best decision for your own circumstances.

Remember, though: if you choose to renew, you're not necessarily committing yourself to the exact same circumstances you've lived in for the past year. You can negotiate certain changes. Check out Option 2 in the next section for more on that, and head back to Section 2.10 for a refresher on your negotiating skills.

Remember: **The earlier you assess your options in terms of renewing or leaving, the more options you'll have.**

5.2

TWO WEEKS BEFORE YOU HAVE TO GIVE NOTICE

You've checked your lease and you know when you need to move out, so it's time to set another date in your calendar: mark the day that is fourteen days before you need to give notice (which is usually thirty or forty-five days before the end of your lease but, as mentioned earlier, can be as much as ninety days before).

Why is that an important date? Roughly two weeks before you need to give notice, here's what you need to be thinking about, in a bit of a choose-your-own-adventure format.

OPTION 1: YOU WANT TO STAY IN YOUR PLACE AND YOUR LEASE RENEWS AUTOMATICALLY

Assuming the terms of the renewal are acceptable to you, then reach out to the landlord at that point to confirm the terms.

This is best done in writing, either via email or text message. Because you're just confirming details of an arrangement that's already in place, it should be a pretty straightforward conversation.

Just let them know that you'd like to stay on and extend the lease, according to the terms of the lease, and they should confirm details with you.

OPTION 2: YOU WANT TO STAY IN YOUR PLACE AND YOUR LEASE DOESN'T AUTOMATICALLY RENEW

Reach out to the landlord and ask about extending for another year.

You've done your homework, so you have a sense of what the rent should be for a place like yours, and now is the time to use that information and suggest to your landlord what you think the rent should be for the year ahead.

Back to the negotiating handbook—this is a concept called "anchoring." Your landlord will have the amount you suggest as a reference point when they think about what the rent should be, and they'll know that if they propose something more, they may have an issue on their hands.

Suggesting a rent level will work well with small landlords, individual landlords in particular. With larger landlords, they will often have a financial model that will spit out a rent number. While it's more challenging to negotiate with larger landlords, it still goes in the "can't hurt, might help" bucket of strategies.

This conversation is best done as just that—a conversation. While you could reach out to them via text or email, it would be best to either talk to them in person or on a phone call.

Your strategy for the conversation can be pretty simple:

1. Thank them for being a great landlord (maybe they were just okay, but sure, go for it—if you're renewing, they couldn't have

been that terrible) and let them know you've enjoyed the place and that you're interested in renewing.

2. Tell them you've done your research and that you have a sense of what the rent should be for the next lease.
3. Propose a new rent number and any other details that are relevant to your situation, which could take into consideration any changes to circumstances—a new pet, a new roommate, a request for a longer lease, etc.

When you're picking a number to offer, remember to be reasonable. We all want to pay less rent, but if you automatically try for lower rent, the landlord is likely to just reject your offer. If you do your research and pick a number that is representative of market rents in the area but one that you could live with, then you should be in good shape.

Remember that rent changes can be substantially different for different areas. Checking out Dwellsy's Rent Maps tool (Dwellsy.com/rent-maps) will give you current rents for your area and will show you how the rent has changed over the past year.

Remember how landlords make money; landlords *hate* turnover. It's expensive and time consuming for them, and they'd rather you stay in the place, assuming you've been at least a reasonable tenant or better, and assuming they can charge you market rent.

So, help them avoid turnover and give them a clear path to what they want, which is for a good renter to stay in the place for another year or longer.

OPTION 3: YOU WANT TO MOVE OUT OF YOUR PLACE

Life happens, plans change, or exciting opportunities present themselves. Or maybe the place just wasn't the right one for you. In any of these cases, it's time to notify your landlord that you're going to move out.

There's a number of moving parts that you want to keep your eye on at this point because you have a few goals to accomplish in this moment:

1. Get as much of your security deposit back as possible
2. Get a good reference from your landlord
3. Understand the move-out procedures for your place

Remember: If you renew and want to negotiate your rent, the key is to do your homework. Have examples of similar places nearby with lower rent to show your landlord.

5.3

HOW TO TELL YOUR LANDLORD YOU'RE MOVING OUT

Of course, you'll have a bunch of different things to get done before the big move, a lot of which we've covered in our earlier sections. In this section, we're going to focus on two different things. The first is what you'll need to do to inform your landlord that you're moving out. The second is how to get back your security deposit—something we know you're eager to do!

Neither of these things should be too difficult, as long as you follow all of the right steps. Let's get started.

CHECK YOUR LEASE

Once you're certain you're going to move out, the first thing you should do is check your lease. There will be instructions there on how to tell your landlord that you're moving out, like how far in advance to let them know and in what form the notice should be given.

NOTICE TO VACATE

A notice to vacate is a letter to your landlord stating your intention to move out. It's pretty straightforward and doesn't require a lawyer or anything fancy. Basically, you'll want to tell them a) that you're moving, b) that you won't be renewing your lease, and c) your planned move-out date.

Here's a handy template for writing your own notice to vacate, which you can also download at Dwellsy.com/blog/how-to-write-a-notice-to-vacate-letter:

[First and Last Name]
[Street Address, Apartment Number]
[City/State/Zip]
Email: [Your Email Address]
[Date]
[Landlord Name]
[Landlord Address]

Dear [Landlord Name],

I've loved living here, but it's time to move. This letter is to provide formal written notice of my intention to vacate my [apartment/home] on [planned move date]. My lease requires [number of days' notice], and here I am giving you even more notice.

If you have any questions or would like to schedule a walkthrough of the apartment, you can reach me at [phone number and/or email address].

I believe that my [apartment/home] is in good condition with normal wear and tear only and look forward to receiving a full refund of my security deposit of [$____]. You can mail it to me here:

[New Address]

Thanks for being a great landlord,

[Your Signature]

[Your Full Name]

Remember: Don't be nervous about serving notice! Your relationship with your landlord is professional. If you act professionally, they will, too.

5.4

HOW TO KEEP AS MUCH OF YOUR SECURITY DEPOSIT AS POSSIBLE

So, how about that security deposit? Remember when you cut that big check when you moved in? You want that money back, right?

Let's help you get all or at least most of it back.

Coming up is a list of tips to make sure that you'll have your entire security deposit refunded to you, but before we get there, let's talk a little about what the security deposit should cover and—importantly—what it should not.

The security deposit is intended to be there as a guarantee that you'll respect the place and treat it like your own, leaving it in substantially the same condition it was in when you moved in.

That said, normal wear and tear happens on any home, and the landlord is responsible for covering those damages—not you. Here are some examples of normal wear and tear:

- **Minor holes in walls from hanging pictures or similar items.** We're talking about pinhole-sized holes in the wall, not big holes.
- **Paint chipping due to age.** Paint generally lasts three to five years, so if yours is that old or older, generalized wear isn't your responsibility.
- **Worn-out carpet.** Wall-to-wall carpets have an expected life of four to seven years, so if they're wearing out or showing the occasional stain, that's something the landlord is responsible for.
- **Blocked plumbing.** Hair and other things flow down the plumbing system and can build up over time, requiring removal. The landlord should take care of this.

You are responsible for any significant damage you may have caused or any lease violations that resulted in costs to the landlord. Here are some examples:

- **Significant pet damage to carpets.** Your cat found a favorite alternative to her litter box? That's your responsibility to fix.
- **Big holes in the walls.** Party got out of control? Dog gnawed through the doorjamb? Movers bashed the hallway walls? Those are your issues, not the landlord's.
- **Inappropriate items in the plumbing.** You know what goes down your drains? Just water and byproducts of cleaning yourself or your things, except when it comes to the toilet—there, it's just bodily waste and toilet paper. Anything else, and you're on the hook. No flushing paper towels, tissues, or anything else, or you might have an expensive mess.

There are areas where there's judgment required on who's responsible, and that's usually where most of the conflict comes between renters and landlords when they're moving out.

For example, the bedroom carpet was new when you moved in two years ago, and it doesn't look great now. Because carpet has an expected life of four to seven years, making it a little on the early side to replace it, who should pay in this instance? This is the kind of thing where you and your landlord have to talk about responsibility, and the answer might be somewhere in the middle, with shared responsibility.

YOUR ACTION PLAN FOR GETTING YOUR SECURITY DEPOSIT BACK

1. **Give Your Notice on Time**
   We've already talked about how there is a clause in your lease about how far in advance to give notice that you're moving out. It's important to give your notice in accordance with what's asked of you in the lease because, otherwise, you could incur a fee. That means that your landlord might keep part of your security deposit in order to compensate for your violation of the lease. The moral of the story is to always make sure you're abiding by the terms of your lease.

2. **Have the Landlord Walk Through After You Give Notice**
   In order to make sure that you haven't missed any damage, you can ask your landlord to do a walkthrough of your apartment after you've given notice. That way, if the landlord flags anything, you two can talk it out right then and there to come up with a solution.

   Before the landlord arrives, make sure to do a thorough cleaning and pick up your stuff. A messy place looks like it's going to have damage hiding somewhere, and a clean place looks like it's ready for the landlord to rent it. Help yourself out by making sure the place looks rentable.

   This walkthrough will give you good information about your landlord's thinking about the condition of the place and prevent any unpleasant surprise deductions from your security deposit—at a time when you still have the ability to address any issues that might cost you.

3. **Make Any Minor Repairs Discussed with the Landlord**
   We know, we know—repairs aren't your thing. But, often, a $3 container of spackle can save you $200 in security-deposit deductions. Look at the things that concerned your landlord and try to take care of any that you can manage.

4. **Clean Your Place—After Your Stuff Is Packed**
   You'll want to make sure your apartment is spotless when you move out. If you leave your apartment dirty, your landlord might keep part of your security deposit in order to pay for professionals to clean your unit after you move out. Instead, you can give the place your own scrub-down before you depart or pay for a team of professional cleaners to do the job for you, both of which could be cheaper than the amount your landlord might hold back from the security deposit.

5. **Make Your Final Payment**
   Make sure to pay your final month's rent before you leave! Yes, some people do forget to do this. Your landlord has the right to deduct unpaid rent from your security deposit if you don't pay it yourself, so ensure that any final payments go through and go through on time. It's best to ask your landlord for confirmation just to be sure that you're all tallied up.

6. **Leave a Forwarding Address**
   You'd be shocked if you knew how many security deposits don't get returned because the landlord can't find the former resident. Make sure you forward your mail with the US Postal Service and give your landlord the address of your new residence so that they're able to send your security deposit back or reach you if there are any concerns about getting it to you.

7. Have the Landlord Walk Through Again Once You've Moved Your Stuff Out

As a final step, it's great to get confirmation from the landlord that the place is as promised and ensure that you've done what you needed to do before handing over the keys. The best way to do this is to have them tour the vacant, clean property so they can look at it without any of your stuff in the way.

8. Take Photos—Lots of Photos

If your landlord says you trashed the carpet but you've already moved out, how do you argue with them? If you have photos of what the place looked like when you left, then you have a basis to argue. If you don't, then you don't.

Make sure you take lots of photos of the place from every angle and in good light so that you can document everything. The best time to do this is after you've cleaned up everything and moved your stuff out. Be sure the photos are date- and time-stamped in your phone settings.

It's also a great practice to send a few representative shots to the landlord at move-out so that you're on the same page about the condition when you departed. This will create a record of the condition of the place at the time when you leave.

9. Turn In Your Key (And Anything Else That's Not Yours)

Yep, this is another one people tend to forget. If you don't turn in your key, your landlord might take the cost of having the locks changed out of your security deposit. Write yourself a reminder to turn your key in.

Plus, remember to return any other items you may have that aren't yours: a garage-door opener, a key to the perimeter fence or to the pool area, etc. If your landlord has their act together, they'll have an inventory of things that have been loaned to you, and they will charge you if you don't return them.

10. Follow Up If Needed

We know you want your security deposit back as soon as possible, and ideally you'd get a check as you walk out the door. That's not the way this works, though.

Security deposits are generally required to be returned within three weeks or a month following your move-out to allow the landlord time to determine any repair costs that might need to be deducted.

If you don't get your security-deposit refund within that time frame, follow up with your previous landlord to make sure it's coming back to you. It's possible that they've forgotten or that they don't have your correct information, so you want to make sure that the deposit gets sent back to you as quickly and smoothly as possible.

Remember: Your security deposit is your money. With a little care for your home and a little bit of work, you can get it back.

5.5

CAN YOU END YOUR LEASE EARLY?

There are tons of reasons why you might have to break your lease early. You might lose your job, have a family emergency, fall ill, or any number of other reasons. It's a time-consuming and financially burdensome situation, but if you have to, you can see it through. We're going to walk you through how to break your lease early if things come to that.

THINGS TO CONSIDER BEFORE YOU BREAK YOUR LEASE

Before we get into the logistics of breaking a lease, you'll want to think carefully about whether it's truly the right decision for you. Here are some things to do before you make the leap:

- **Calculate the financial consequences.** Breaking your lease can be an expensive undertaking. You'll probably have to pay a penalty, and that could be worth as much as two months' rent plus your security deposit.

- **Assess your situation.** You might have legal grounds for breaking your lease, such as if the rental property is uninhabitable, your landlord has breached your lease, or your rental is in terrible condition. Make sure to check out the conditions of a legal lease break and see if you meet them.
- **Read through your lease.** If there is a section about lease termination in your lease, find it and read it over to see what it says about legal lease termination. The section might contain complex legal jargon; in that case, make sure you understand it before you proceed. If there is no section about lease termination in your lease, then move on to talking to your landlord.
- **Talk to your landlord.** Get in touch with your landlord as soon as you can in order to explain to them why you want to break your lease. Be honest, transparent, and exact—you want your landlord to know precisely why and when you'd like to break your lease. If you're lucky, they might let you leave without a penalty.

HOW TO BREAK YOUR LEASE

Okay, so you've decided to take the jump—you want to break your lease. Good luck! Here are a few of the next steps and some of the options you might be able to work out with your landlord.

Gather Your Documents

If the reason that you're breaking your lease is something you've documented, you'll want to get all of your evidence together. This could be something like a medical condition that you want to prove to your landlord. However, it could also be something like the rental being in terrible condition. In that case, you'll want to have evidence of the ways that the rental is uninhabitable, so make sure to take pictures and make notes of any correspondence you have with your landlord about the problems in the rental. In this situation, you may also need legal advice or help from a local tenant advocate. Check Dwellsy.com/blog/rentersorganizations for options.

Work Out a Deal with Your Landlord

At some point, you will have to sit down and talk to your landlord if you haven't already done so. It's possible that you can negotiate a deal, like offering to pay a penalty fee or helping the landlord find a new tenant. You could also offer to buy out your lease, which means that you would pay a certain amount of money for your landlord to release you from your rental contract.

Subletting

Some leases have clauses about subletting. A subletter is someone who occupies your rental when you're away. This is a good option if you only want to leave for a short amount of time, although a subletter can also take over for the rest of your tenancy. If there is no clause about subletting in your lease, you'll have to talk to your landlord about it and see if they agree. It's important to remember that you'll be held responsible for any damages or defaults the subletter makes. For example, if they don't pay the rent, then you'll have to. If they damage the place, it'll be your responsibility to pay for repairs.

Military Release

The Servicemembers Civil Relief Act (SCRA) allows you to end your lease early if you've received orders requiring you to begin active-duty service in another location. You must have a service duration of at least ninety days, and you'll have to give your landlord a copy of your orders and, if possible, thirty days' notice. Your lease will end thirty days after your next monthly rent payment is due.

Lease Assignment

A lease assignment is similar to a sublet in that you're handing your lease over to someone else. However, the two are different because you don't have any responsibilities under a lease assignment. A sublet is only temporary, whereas a lease assignment means that you're permanently moving out and don't plan to return. You'll have to talk to your landlord about a lease assignment to get their consent to go forward with this option.

Completing the Lease Term

If the reason you're moving out can wait and you can't reach an agreement with your landlord, it's best to just complete your lease term. It's the last option, but it's always there.

END YOUR LEASE ON GOOD TERMS

Whatever your reasons for wanting to break your lease, try to end on good terms with your landlord. You'll avoid legal repercussions and any bad referrals or personal feelings that way. Your best bet is just to be clear, honest, and courteous throughout the entire process.

Remember: Breaking your lease early can be a difficult and stressful process, but it's not impossible. Work with your landlord to find an outcome that makes both of you happy.

Things to Remember

If you're a recent purchaser of this book, that probably means you have one of the biggest life decisions in front of you: where to live. We wrote this book because when we were in your shoes, we wished we had a resource just like this.

There is a lot of content and advice in this book—more than most can absorb in a single reading. That's because this process can be challenging and complex to navigate, even at the best of times.

But we'd like you to hear this: *you can do it.*

It's not going to be perfect, and you'll get better at it with time, but with this book in hand, you have all the information you need to do an amazing search and get yourself a great home.

Here are some of our top tips for having a great search and making the most of this book:

1. **Be first.** We cannot say this often enough. You need to be the first to inquire, the first to apply, and the first to put your money down. Know where you are in the landlord's process, and if there's a line of folks who got there before you, move on to the next rental and don't waste your time.
2. **Be safe.** Sadly, scammers are out to get you in the search. As we mentioned in Section 1.5, over 20 percent of renters get scammed in the search process. Let's put the scammers out of business by being careful in the search.

3. **Know what you want.** If you know what you're looking for, your search is going to be that much more effective. Knowing what you want—and, just as importantly, what you do not want—is a superpower in this process. Take the time to really evaluate what would make a place right for you.
4. **Keep this book nearby.** There are a lot of unique situations covered in this book, and depending on your search, any number of them could present themselves. Keep this book handy and use it as a reference when you need it.

All of us here at Dwellsy are rooting for you. Good luck in the search, and let us know how it goes. You can find us at Dwellsy.com/everythingrenting, and we look forward to hearing from you.

Acknowledgments

Writing a book like this in so many ways wraps together all the experiences I've had in my life thus far, and there are so many amazing people who have helped me along the way.

I'm grateful to the amazing team at Dwellsy that has built an incredible service for renters and landlords and, in doing so, has made this book possible. Chudi Anyaeche, Andrea Childress, Matt Greene, Livia Hansen, Nikolay Ivanov, Lily Medeiros, Barry Melton, Yana Moskalova, Michael Pedersen, Lena Stevens, Jeremy Washington, and Garrett Zuiderweg, thank you. I'm so very lucky to work with each of you.

I wouldn't be here and in a position to write a book like this without all those from whom I've had the chance to learn over the years, and of course I have to start with those who have taught me about real estate and renting. The list is extraordinarily long, and there isn't room to do justice to it here, but some of those who have been most generous in teaching me the ins and outs of the business are: Josh Anbil, Louise Austin, Adam Berry, Chuck Burd, John Burkart, Richard Crofts, Remco Daal, Regina Eugea, Cheryl Gray, Kelly Hales, Michael Herzberg, Bill Krauch, Toby Pennycuff, Sarah Postyn, Chas Nardoni, Bill Ferguson, Tim Kessler, Mike McKee, Lawrence Neilson, Doug Poutasse, Amy Price, Donna Ashley Rich, Lydia Tan, and Gary Whitelaw. Thank you all.

Among amazing real-estate leaders who have taught me so much through the years, Christa Leary and Donje Putnam stand out, not just because of their excellence but also for their willingness to step up as readers of the manuscript. This book is far better for your work. Thank you.

I tell stories about site visits constantly, and I would be remiss if I didn't thank the hundreds of property-management professionals at Essex Property Trust and other companies who took time out of their very busy days to spend time with me in one way or another. I owe a particular shout-out to those who let me shadow them for entire days and those who put up with me mystery shopping their properties and didn't rat me out if they knew who I was.

So many others have helped me along the way, and I'll always be grateful to them for their help, mentorship, and coaching. Glenn Farrell, Chris Fix, Josh Hinerfeld, Barak Kassar, Mary Rawlinson, and Jim Tallman—thank you to all of you. I wouldn't be who I am today without your leadership, guidance, and mentorship.

We wouldn't have been able to build Dwellsy and bring renters all of this amazing information without the steadfast support and counsel from a great group of investors, including Michael Fertik and Matt Robinson of Heroic Ventures; Ajay Singh of Frontiers Capital; Miriam Rivera, Clint Korver, and Steve Reale of Ulu Ventures; Joanna Rupp of the University of Chicago; John Schuster, Peter Lukens, and Nawaf Bitar of NPJ Ventures; Bob Burke, Curtis Feeny, and John Barton of the Stanford Farmers; and Ray Levitt of Blackhorn Ventures.

This book would not have been in any way possible without those who helped me though every step of this journey. That journey begins with my coauthor, Hannah Hildebolt, who brought incredible talent, perspective, and voice, balancing out the "voice of experience" with the perspective of the new renter. We wouldn't be here without the kindness of a stranger, Erin Edmison, who took a cold call from a fellow Vassar alum and educated me on how the book business works. I'll be forever grateful for Matt Wagner, the literary agent who was willing to listen to a new idea and quickly became a believer; for Matt Holt, the publisher who jumped in and took a chance on us without hesitation; and for Katie Dickman, our amazing editor, Brigid Pearson and Kim Broderick, the designers who, along with Dwellsy's own Garrett Zuiderweg, made the book look great, and the whole BenBella/Matt Holt team.

Of course, none of this would have been possible without my partner in all things, Rosalind. She is my wife, my cofounder at Dwellsy, the mother to our three amazing children, and my perfect complement. Every day, I wake up and go to sleep grateful that we found each other.

—Jonas

Ever since I was small, I've dreamed of having my writing published. When I joined Dwellsy, I had no idea that my work for the company would lead to this book. So my first thanks have to go to Jonas, who brought me on board in the first place. Jonas is not only my coauthor and my boss; he is my mentor, too. He is a source of endless kindness and patience. While I was juggling this book and my master's dissertation, Jonas never rushed me. He only encouraged me and asked what he could do to help. On every single one of our calls together, his first question is always "How are you?" and he listens when I answer. He is a true leader and a man who cares about Dwellsy's employees as human beings.

I'd also like to thank Dwellsy's entire hardworking and dedicated team. They care so much about what we're building together, and it's an honor to work alongside them. Particularly, I'd like to thank Lena Stevens, one of my best friends and the staffer who suggested that I write for Dwellsy.

Of course, I have to thank the teams at BenBella/Matt Holt because this would not have been possible without them. I'll cosign everything Jonas said with regard to these folks, with my own special thanks to Katie Dickman for answering all of my questions as I stumbled through the publishing process.

Many people were kind enough to read portions of this book and make it way better. These are generally the same people who I turned to when I was stressed or frazzled, so I'll recognize them for both. Thanks on this score are due to Daphne Kwon (my mom), Bill Hildebolt (my dad), Hazen Hildebolt (my brother), Léa Machado Formiga (my partner), Nika McKechnie, Emily Frank, Rui Cheng, Ella Xiao, Abrianna Harris, Matisse Peppet, Skylar Karzhevsky, Jo Zenn, Max Wagh, and ZB Senft.

All of my grandparents have lent their support to my writing in too many ways to name. Thanks to Sandi Hildebolt (my nana), William Hildebolt (my late grandpa), Taek Joon Kwon (my late papa), and Moon Ja Kwon (my late *halmeoni*). Thank you for all of your encouragement and your never-ending belief in your granddaughter's abilities. I love you very much.

—Hannah

Endnotes

1 Emily Starbuck Crone and Daniel Tonkovich, "How Much More It Costs to Own vs. Rent in Your State," NerdWallet (blog), March 22, 2017, https://www.nerdwallet.com/article/mortgages/cost-homeownership-vs-renting.

2 Roy Maurer, "Americans Most Often Move for Work," *Society for Human Resource Management* (blog), May 2, 2017, https://www.shrm.org/resourcesandtools/hr-topics/talent-acquisition/pages/americans-most-often-move-work.aspx.

3 Mihaela Buzec, "What Are Apartment Utilities and How Much Will They Cost Me?" RentCafe (blog), July 12, 2022, https://www.rentcafe.com/blog/apartment-search-2/money/apartment-utilities-breakdown/#water.

4 "Fair Housing: Wisconsin," National Apartment Association, March 2022, https://www.naahq.org/fair-housing-wisconsin.

5 "Housing Discrimination Under the Fair Housing Act," HUD.gov, US Department of Housing and Urban Development (HUD), accessed December 19, 2022, https://www.hud.gov/program_offices/fair_housing_equal_opp/fair_housing_act_overview.

6 "Federal Rental Assistance Fact Sheets," Center on Budget and Policy Priorities, January 19, 2022, https://www.cbpp.org/research/housing/federal-rental-assistance-fact-sheets#US.

7 "Chicago Alderwoman Waits 29 Years for Housing Assistance, Takes Legislative Action for Change," WBAL.com, July 1, 2022, https://www.wbal.com/article/573095/110/chicago-alderwoman-waits-29-years-for-housing-assistance-takes-legislative-action-for-change.

Index

D

M

N

O

P

About the Authors

Jonas Bordo is the CEO and cofounder of Dwellsy and has been around the rental business for many years. He's been a renter many, many times and has some crazy stories to tell, and he's been a landlord, too, both on a small scale and a huge scale—he was once responsible for sixty thousand apartments. He's taken that insider knowledge and put it to use to build Dwellsy, the nation's preeminent marketplace for rental housing, and to help renters get an edge and find a great place to live more quickly, more easily, and more safely.

Hannah Hildebolt is a staff writer for Dwellsy. Her writing has simplified the complex world of real estate for Dwellsy's nationwide audience of renters. Hannah recently returned to the United States after studying abroad in Scotland, where she earned a master's degree in English literature. She currently resides in New York City.

Dwellsy Has Another Gift For You

This book equipped you with the essential knowledge to be a successful renter. The rental market can be a scary place, so we want to make sure you're as equipped and protected as possible. That's why we developed Dwellsy Edge.

Dwellsy Edge is a digital service that provides renters with the tools to overcome common apartment-hunting challenges. Dwellsy Edge truly gives you the edge over other renters by increasing your chances of getting your rental application seen first, improving your search criteria, and protecting you from rental fraud.

Find your ideal home in no time! Visit www.dwellsy.com/dwellsy-edge and enter EYNTK2023 to get 25% off Dwellsy Edge.

"Pairing *Everything You Need to Know About Renting* with Dwellsy Edge helped me find my next home with ease."
—Satisfied Dwellsy Edge User